WILLIAM SHAKESPEARE was born in Stratford-upon-Avon in April, 1564, and his birth is traditionally celebrated on April 23. The facts of his life, known from surviving documents, are sparse. He was one of eight children born to John Shakespeare, a merchant of some standing in his community. William probably went to the King's New School in Stratford, but he had no university education. In November 1582, at the age of eighteen, he married Anne Hathaway, eight years his senior, who was pregnant with their first child, Susanna. She was born on May 26, 1583. Twins, a boy, Hamnet (who would die at age eleven), and a girl, Judith, were born in 1585. By 1592 Shakespeare had gone to London, working as an actor and already known as a playwright. A rival dramatist, Robert Greene, referred to him as "an upstart crow, beautified with our feathers." Shakespeare became a principal shareholder and playwright of the successful acting troupe the Lord Chamberlain's men (later, under James I, called the King's men). In 1599 the Lord Chamberlain's men built and occupied the Globe Theatre in Southwark near the Thames River. Here many of Shakespeare's plays were performed by the most famous actors of his time, including Richard Burbage, Will Kempe, and Robert Armin. In addition to his 37 plays, Shakespeare had a hand in others, including *Sir Thomas More* and *The Two Noble Kinsmen*, and he wrote poems, including *Venus and Adonis* and *The Rape of Lucrece*. His 154 sonnets were published, probably without his authorization, in 1609. In 1611 or 1612 he gave up his lodgings in London and devoted more and more of his time to retirement in Stratford, though he continued writing such plays as *The Tempest* and *Henry VIII* until about 1613. He died on April 23, 1616, and was buried in Holy Trinity Church, Stratford. No collected edition of his plays was published during his lifetime, but in 1623 two members of his acting company, John Heminges and Henry Condell, published the great collection now called the First Folio.

**Bantam Shakespeare
The Complete Works—29 Volumes
Edited by David Bevington
With forewords by Joseph Papp on the plays**

The Poems: Venus and Adonis, The Rape of Lucrece, The
Phoenix and Turtle, A Lover's Complaint,
the Sonnets

Antony and Cleopatra	*The Merchant of Venice*
As You Like It	*A Midsummer Night's Dream*
The Comedy of Errors	*Much Ado about Nothing*
Hamlet	*Othello*
Henry IV, Part One	*Richard II*
Henry IV, Part Two	*Richard III*
Henry V	*Romeo and Juliet*
Julius Caesar	*The Taming of the Shrew*
King Lear	*The Tempest*
Macbeth	*Twelfth Night*

Together in one volume:

Henry VI, Parts One, Two, and Three
King John and Henry VIII
Measure for Measure, All's Well that Ends Well, and·.
Troilus and Cressida
Three Early Comedies: Love's Labor's Lost, The Two
Gentlemen of Verona, The Merry
Wives of Windsor
Three Classical Tragedies: Titus Andronicus, Timon
of Athens, Coriolanus
The Late Romances: Pericles, Cymbeline, The Winter's
Tale, The Tempest

Two collections:

Four Comedies: The Taming of the Shrew, A Midsummer
Night's Dream, The Merchant of Venice,
Twelfth Night
Four Tragedies: Hamlet, Othello, King Lear, Macbeth

William Shakespeare

OTHELLO

Edited by
David Bevington

David Scott Kastan,
James Hammersmith,
and Robert Kean Turner,
Associate Editors

With a Foreword by
Joseph Papp

BANTAM BOOKS

NEW YORK · TORONTO · LONDON · SYDNEY · AUCKLAND

OTHELLO

*A Bantam Book / published by arrangement
with Scott, Foresman and Company*

PUBLISHING HISTORY

*Scott, Foresman edition published / January 1980
Bantam edition, with newly edited text and substantially revised, edited,
and amplified notes, introductions, and other materials,
published / February 1988
Valuable advice on staging matters has been provided by Richard Hosley.
Collations checked by Eric Rasmussen.
Additional editorial assistance by Claire McEachern.*

ISBN 0-553-21302-4

Published simultaneously in the United States and Canada

PRINTED IN THE UNITED STATES OF AMERICA

O   20 19 18 17 16

Contents

Foreword

It's hard to imagine, but Shakespeare wrote all of his plays with a quill pen, a goose feather whose hard end had to be sharpened frequently. How many times did he scrape the dull end to a point with his knife, dip it into the inkwell, and bring up, dripping wet, those wonderful words and ideas that are known all over the world?

In the age of word processors, typewriters, and ballpoint pens, we have almost forgotten the meaning of the word "blot." Yet when I went to school, in the 1930s, my classmates and I knew all too well what an inkblot from the metal-tipped pens we used would do to a nice clean page of a test paper, and we groaned whenever a splotch fell across the sheet. Most of us finished the school day with ink-stained fingers; those who were less careful also went home with ink-stained shirts, which were almost impossible to get clean.

When I think about how long it took me to write the simplest composition with a metal-tipped pen and ink, I can only marvel at how many plays Shakespeare scratched out with his goose-feather quill pen, year after year. Imagine him walking down one of the narrow cobblestoned streets of London, or perhaps drinking a pint of beer in his local alehouse. Suddenly his mind catches fire with an idea, or a sentence, or a previously elusive phrase. He is burning with impatience to write it down—but because he doesn't have a ballpoint pen or even a pencil in his pocket, he has to keep the idea in his head until he can get to his quill and parchment.

He rushes back to his lodgings on Silver Street, ignoring the vendors hawking brooms, the coaches clattering by, the piteous wails of beggars and prisoners. Bounding up the stairs, he snatches his quill and starts to write furiously, not even bothering to light a candle against the dusk. "To be, or not to be," he scrawls, "that is the—." But the quill point has gone dull, the letters have fattened out illegibly, and in the middle of writing one of the most famous passages in the history of dramatic literature, Shakespeare has to stop to sharpen his pen.

Taking a deep breath, he lights a candle now that it's dark, sits down, and begins again. By the time the candle has burned out and the noisy apprentices of his French Huguenot landlord have quieted down, Shakespeare has finished Act 3 of *Hamlet* with scarcely a blot.

Early the next morning, he hurries through the fog of a London summer morning to the rooms of his colleague Richard Burbage, the actor for whom the role of Hamlet is being written. He finds Burbage asleep and snoring loudly, sprawled across his straw mattress. Not only had the actor performed in *Henry V* the previous afternoon, but he had then gone out carousing all night with some friends who had come to the performance.

Shakespeare shakes his friend awake, until, bleary-eyed, Burbage sits up in his bed. "Dammit, Will," he grumbles, "can't you let an honest man sleep?" But the playwright, his eyes shining and the words tumbling out of his mouth, says, "Shut up and listen—tell me what you think of *this*!"

He begins to read to the still half-asleep Burbage, pacing around the room as he speaks. ". . . Whether 'tis nobler in the mind to suffer the slings and arrows of outrageous fortune—"

Burbage interrupts, suddenly wide awake, "That's excellent, very good, 'the slings and arrows of outrageous fortune,' yes, I think it will work quite well. . . ." He takes the parchment from Shakespeare and murmurs the lines to himself, slowly at first but with growing excitement.

The sun is just coming up, and the words of one of Shakespeare's most famous soliloquies are being uttered for the first time by the first actor ever to bring Hamlet to life. It must have been an exhilarating moment.

Shakespeare wrote most of his plays to be performed live by the actor Richard Burbage and the rest of the Lord Chamberlain's men (later the King's men). Today, however, our first encounter with the plays is usually in the form of the printed word. And there is no question that reading Shakespeare for the first time isn't easy. His plays aren't comic books or magazines or the dime-store detective novels I read when I was young. A lot of his sentences are complex. Many of his words are no longer used in our everyday speech. His profound thoughts are often condensed into poetry, which is not as straightforward as prose.

Yet when you hear the words spoken aloud, a lot of the language may strike you as unexpectedly modern. For Shakespeare's plays, like any dramatic work, weren't really meant to be read; they were meant to be spoken, seen, and performed. It's amazing how lines that are so troublesome in print can flow so naturally and easily when spoken.

I think it was precisely this music that first fascinated me. When I was growing up, Shakespeare was a stranger to me. I had no particular interest in him, for I was from a different cultural tradition. It never occurred to me that his plays might be more than just something to "get through" in school, like science or math or the physical education requirement we had to fulfill. My passions then were movies, radio, and vaudeville—certainly not Elizabethan drama.

I was, however, fascinated by words and language. Because I grew up in a home where Yiddish was spoken, and English was only a second language, I was acutely sensitive to the musical sounds of different languages and had an ear for lilt and cadence and rhythm in the spoken word. And so I loved reciting poems and speeches even as a very young child. In first grade I learned lots of short nature verses—"Who has seen the wind?," one of them began. My first foray into drama was playing the role of Scrooge in Charles Dickens's *A Christmas Carol* when I was eight years old. I liked summoning all the scorn and coldness I possessed and putting them into the words, "Bah, humbug!"

From there I moved on to longer and more famous poems and other works by writers of the 1930s. Then, in junior high school, I made my first acquaintance with Shakespeare through his play *Julius Caesar*. Our teacher, Miss McKay, assigned the class a passage to memorize from the opening scene of the play, the one that begins "Wherefore rejoice? What conquest brings he home?" The passage seemed so wonderfully theatrical and alive to me, and the experience of memorizing and reciting it was so much fun, that I went on to memorize another speech from the play on my own.

I chose Mark Antony's address to the crowd in Act 3,

scene 2, which struck me then as incredibly high drama.
Even today, when I speak the words, I feel the same thrill I
did that first time. There is the strong and athletic Antony
descending from the raised pulpit where he has been speaking, right into the midst of a crowded Roman square. Hold-
ing the torn and bloody cloak of the murdered Julius
Caesar in his hand, he begins to speak to the people of
Rome:

> If you have tears, prepare to shed them now.
> You all do know this mantle. I remember   .
> The first time ever Caesar put it on;
> 'Twas on a summer's evening in his tent,
> That day he overcame the Nervii.
> Look, in this place ran Cassius' dagger through.
> See what a rent the envious Casca made.
> Through this the well-belovèd Brutus stabbed,
> And as he plucked his cursèd steel away,
> Mark how the blood of Caesar followed it,
> As rushing out of doors to be resolved
> If Brutus so unkindly knocked or no;
> For Brutus, as you know, was Caesar's angel.
> Judge, O you gods, how dearly Caesar loved him!
> This was the most unkindest cut of all . . .

I'm not sure now that I even knew Shakespeare had written a lot of other plays, or that he was considered "time-
less," "universal," or "classic"—but I knew a good speech
when I heard one, and I found the splendid rhythms of
Antony's rhetoric as exciting as anything I'd ever come
across.

Fifty years later, I still feel that way. Hearing good actors
speak Shakespeare gracefully and naturally is a wonderful
experience, unlike any other I know. There's a satisfying
fullness to the spoken word that the printed page just can't
convey. This is why seeing the plays of Shakespeare performed live in a theater is the best way to appreciate them.
If you can't do that, listening to sound recordings or watching film versions of the plays is the next best thing.

But if you do start with the printed word, use the play as a
script. Be an actor yourself and say the lines out loud. Don't
worry too much at first about words you don't immediately
understand. Look them up in the footnotes or a dictionary,

but don't spend too much time on this. It is more profitable (and fun) to get the sense of a passage and sing it out. Speak naturally, almost as if you were talking to a friend, but be sure to enunciate the words properly. You'll be surprised at how much you understand simply by speaking the speech "trippingly on the tongue," as Hamlet advises the Players.

You might start, as I once did, with a speech from *Julius Caesar*, in which the tribune (city official) Marullus scolds the commoners for transferring their loyalties so quickly from the defeated and murdered general Pompey to the newly victorious Julius Caesar:

> Wherefore rejoice? What conquest brings he home?
> What tributaries follow him to Rome
> To grace in captive bonds his chariot wheels?
> You blocks, you stones, you worse than senseless
>   things!
> O you hard hearts, you cruel men of Rome,
> Knew you not Pompey? Many a time and oft
> Have you climbed up to walls and battlements,
> To towers and windows, yea, to chimney tops,
> Your infants in your arms, and there have sat
> The livelong day, with patient expectation,
> To see great Pompey pass the streets of Rome.

With the exception of one or two words like "wherefore" (which means "why," not "where"), "tributaries" (which means "captives"), and "patient expectation" (which means patient waiting), the meaning and emotions of this speech can be easily understood.

From here you can go on to dialogues or other more challenging scenes. Although you may stumble over unaccustomed phrases or unfamiliar words at first, and even fall flat when you're crossing some particularly rocky passages, pick yourself up and stay with it. Remember that it takes time to feel at home with anything new. Soon you'll come to recognize Shakespeare's unique sense of humor and way of saying things as easily as you recognize a friend's laughter.

And then it will just be a matter of choosing which one of Shakespeare's plays you want to tackle next. As a true fan of his, you'll find that you're constantly learning from his plays. It's a journey of discovery that you can continue for the rest of your life. For no matter how many times you read or see a particular play, there will always be something new there that you won't have noticed before.

Why do so many thousands of people get hooked on Shakespeare and develop a habit that lasts a lifetime? What can he really say to us today, in a world filled with inventions and problems he never could have imagined? And how do you get past his special language and difficult sentence structure to understand him?

The best way to answer these questions is to go see a live production. You might not know much about Shakespeare, or much about the theater, but when you watch actors performing one of his plays on the stage, it will soon become clear to you why people get so excited about a playwright who lived hundreds of years ago.

For the story—what's happening in the play—is the most accessible part of Shakespeare. In *A Midsummer Night's Dream*, for example, you can immediately understand the situation: a girl is chasing a guy who's chasing a girl who's chasing another guy. No wonder *A Midsummer Night's Dream* is one of the most popular of Shakespeare's plays: it's about one of the world's most popular pastimes— falling in love.

But the course of true love never did run smooth, as the young suitor Lysander says. Often in Shakespeare's comedies the girl whom the guy loves doesn't love him back, or she loves him but he loves someone else. In *The Two Gentlemen of Verona*, Julia loves Proteus, Proteus loves Sylvia, and Sylvia loves Valentine, who is Proteus's best friend. In the end, of course, true love prevails, but not without lots of complications along the way.

For in all of his plays—comedies, histories, and tragedies—Shakespeare is showing you human nature. His characters act and react in the most extraordinary ways—and sometimes in the most incomprehensible ways. People are always trying to find motivations for what a character does. They ask, "Why does Iago want to destroy Othello?"

The answer, to me, is very simple—because that's the way Iago is. That's just his nature. Shakespeare doesn't explain his characters; he sets them in motion—and away they go. He doesn't worry about whether they're likable or not. He's interested in interesting people, and his most fascinating characters are those who are unpredictable. If you lean back in your chair early on in one of his plays, thinking you've figured out what Iago or Shylock (in *The Merchant of Venice*) is up to, don't be too sure—because that great judge of human nature, Shakespeare, will surprise you every time.

He is just as wily in the way he structures a play. In *Macbeth*, a comic scene is suddenly introduced just after the bloodiest and most treacherous slaughter imaginable, of a guest and king by his host and subject, when in comes a drunk porter who has to go to the bathroom. Shakespeare is tickling your emotions by bringing a stand-up comic on-stage right on the heels of a savage murder.

It has taken me thirty years to understand even some of these things, and so I'm not suggesting that Shakespeare is immediately understandable. I've gotten to know him not through theory but through practice, the practice of the *living* Shakespeare—the playwright of the theater.

Of course the plays are a great achievement of dramatic literature, and they should be studied and analyzed in schools and universities. But you must always remember, when reading all the words *about* the playwright and his plays, that *Shakespeare's* words came first and that in the end there is nothing greater than a single actor on the stage speaking the lines of Shakespeare.

Everything important that I know about Shakespeare comes from the practical business of producing and directing his plays in the theater. The task of classifying, criticizing, and editing Shakespeare's printed works I happily leave to others. For me, his plays really do live on the stage, not on the page. That is what he wrote them for and that is how they are best appreciated.

Although Shakespeare lived and wrote hundreds of years ago, his name rolls off my tongue as if he were my brother. As a producer and director, I feel that there is a professional relationship between us that spans the centuries. As a human being, I feel that Shakespeare has enriched my understanding of life immeasurably. I hope you'll let him do the same for you.

❖

Othello is filled with extraordinary characters and speeches. There's Othello himself, with his blind and fatal trust in the wrong people. There's the remarkably strong Desdemona, whose defiance of her father to marry Othello would have been exceptional for that time. Lieutenant Cassio plays a vital role as the instrument employed by Iago to feed Othello's jealousy by winning Desdemona's sympathy.

And of course, Iago is Shakespeare's ultimate villain, that fiendishly smooth serpent of a man. I see him as a graceful, slender, elegant type, sophisticated, and, like Richard III, totally devoid of any moral sense. Possessed of that fine-tuned awareness of other people's weaknesses that psychopathic people often have, Iago knows precisely where to prick Othello. Slowly and surely, he moves in for the kill; we marvel at his finesse and subtlety as we watch.

How he does it—and not why—is what makes the play interesting. Iago himself gives several reasons for his hatred of the Moor—Iago wasn't promoted, he suspects Othello of sleeping with his wife, he loves Othello's wife Desdemona—but in the end none of these really account for what he does. He has the capacity to create the right circumstances, and then he makes them work for his purposes.

To all of these characters Shakespeare brings his amazing powers of perception as he examines a variety of human natures. We recognize Othello, or Desdemona, or Cassio, because we've seen them recreated countless times in ourselves and in other people—people who are jealous, or unfairly accused, or unwitting victims of someone else's cruelty. There's nothing in Shakespeare that isn't within the realm of human possibility. His characters aren't false, soap opera versions of real people; they *are* real people.

As in all of his plays, Shakespeare wrote some extraordinary speeches for *Othello*. Cassio's heartbroken outcry in Act 2, scene 3, about his reputation—in contrast to Falstaff's disdaining of "honor" as a mere word—is one example. Othello's explanation to the Venetian senators of how he and Desdemona fell in love, as he told her the story of his life, is gorgeously eloquent:

> She thanked me,
> And bade me, if I had a friend that loved her,
> I should but teach him how to tell my story
> And that would woo her. Upon this hint I spake.
> She loved me for the dangers I had passed,
> And I loved her that she did pity them.

The frank, surprisingly contemporary discussion Desdemona and Emilia have about marriage and infidelity, in Act 4, scene 3, has always been a favorite of mine.

DESDEMONA
    Dost thou in conscience think—tell me, Emilia—
    That there be women do abuse their husbands
    In such gross kind?
EMILIA   There be some such, no question.
DESDEMONA
    Wouldst thou do such a deed for all the world?
EMILIA
    Why, would not you?
DESDEMONA   No, by this heavenly light!
EMILIA
    Nor I neither by this heavenly light;
    I might do 't as well i' the dark.
DESDEMONA
    Wouldst thou do such a deed for all the world?
EMILIA
    The world's a huge thing. It is a great price
    For a small vice.
DESDEMONA
    Good troth, I think thou wouldst not.

Throughout this scene, Emilia's worldliness is contrasted to Desdemona's utter innocence and faith, which Shakespeare deliberately emphasizes shortly before Othello comes in to murder her. It's an ingenious dramatic prelude to the crime.

Othello's murder of Desdemona is one of Shakespeare's great scenes, though it can cause a slight problem for the director, who has to figure out how Desdemona can speak after she's been throttled. If not handled gingerly, this can easily lead to laughter, which will obviously destroy the delicate pathos of the scene. Nineteenth-century producers often solved the problem by having Othello stab Desdemona with a dagger instead of smothering her, but I consider that a coward's way out.

In a moving conclusion to the tragedy, before he takes his own life, Othello utters the poignant speech that begins, "Soft you; a word or two before you go":

> I pray you, in your letters,
> When you shall these unlucky deeds relate,
> Speak of me as I am; nothing extenuate,
> Nor set down aught in malice. Then must you speak
> Of one that loved not wisely but too well.

Othello is such a rich play, with its characters drawn straight from life and its array of gorgeous speeches, that it deserves to be read and performed over and over—as does all of Shakespeare.

JOSEPH PAPP

JOSEPH PAPP GRATEFULLY ACKNOWLEDGES THE HELP OF ELIZABETH KIRKLAND IN PREPARING THIS FOREWORD.

OTHELLO

Introduction

Othello differs in several respects from the other three major Shakespearean tragedies with which it is usually ranked. Written seemingly about the time of its performance at court by the King's men (Shakespeare's acting company) on November 1, 1604, after *Hamlet* (c. 1599–1601) and before *King Lear* (c. 1605) and *Macbeth* (c. 1606–1607), *Othello* shares with these other plays a fascination with evil in its most virulent and universal aspect. These plays study the devastating effects of ambitious pride, ingratitude, wrath, jealousy, and vengeful hate—the deadly sins of the spirit—with only a passing interest in the political strife to which Shakespeare's Roman or classical tragedies are generally devoted. Of the four, *Othello* is the most concentrated upon one particular evil. The action concerns sexual jealousy, and although human sinfulness is such that jealousy ceaselessly touches on other forms of depravity, the center of interest always returns in *Othello* to the destruction of a love through jealousy. *Othello* is a tragic portrait of a marriage. The protagonist is not a king or prince, as in the tragedies already mentioned, but a general recently married. There are no supernatural visitations as in *Hamlet* and *Macbeth*. Ideas of divine justice, while essential to *Othello*'s portrayal of a battle between good and evil for the allegiance of the protagonist, do not encompass the wide sweep of *King Lear;* nor do we find here the same broad indictment of humanity. Social order is not seriously shaken by Othello's tragedy. The fair-minded Duke of Venice remains firmly in control, and his deputy Lodovico oversees a just conclusion on Cyprus.

By the same token, *Othello* does not offer the remorseless questioning about man's relationship to the cosmos that we find in *King Lear, Hamlet,* and *Macbeth*. The battle of good and evil is of course cosmic, but in *Othello* that battle is realized through a taut narrative of jealousy and murder. Its poetic images are accordingly focused to a large extent on the natural world. One cluster of images is domestic and animal, having to do with goats, monkeys, wolves, baboons, guinea hens, wildcats, spiders, flies, asses, dogs, copulating horses and sheep, serpents, and toads; other images, more wide-ranging in scope, include green-eyed monsters, devils, blackness, poisons, money purses, tarnished jewels, music untuned, and light extinguished. The story is immediate and direct, retaining the sensational atmosphere of its Italian prose source by Giovanni Baptista Giraldi Cinthio, in his *Hecatommithi* of 1565 (translated into French in 1584). Events move even more swiftly than in Cinthio, for Shakespeare has compressed the story into two or three nights and days (albeit with an intervening sea journey and with an elastic use of stage time to allow for the maturing of long-term plans, as when we learn that Iago has begged Emilia "a hundred times" to steal Desdemona's handkerchief, or that Iago has accused Cassio of making love to Desdemona "a thousand times"). *Othello* does not have a fully developed double plot as in *King Lear* or a comparatively large group of characters serving as foils to the protagonist as in *Hamlet*. *Othello*'s cast is small and the plot is concentrated to an unusual degree on Othello, Desdemona, and Iago. What *Othello* may lose in breadth it gains in dramatic intensity.

Daringly, Shakespeare opens this tragedy of love not with a direct and sympathetic portrayal of the lovers themselves, but with a scene of vicious insinuation about their marriage. The images employed by Iago to describe the coupling of Othello and Desdemona are revoltingly animalistic, sodomistic. "Even now, now, very now, an old black ram / Is tupping your white ewe," he taunts Desdemona's father Brabantio. ("Tupping" is a word used specifically for the copulating of sheep.) "You'll have your daughter covered with a Barbary horse; you'll have your nephews neigh to you"; "your daughter and the Moor are now making the beast with two backs"; "the devil will make a grandsire of you" (1.1.90–93, 113–120). This degraded view reduces the marriage to one of utter carnality, with repeated emphasis on the word "gross": Desdemona has yielded "to the gross clasps of a lascivious Moor," and has made "a gross revolt" against her family and society (ll. 129, 137). Iago's second theme, one that is habitual with him, is money. "What ho, Brabantio! Thieves, thieves, thieves! / Look to your house, your daughter, and your bags!" (ll. 81–82). The implication is of a sinister bond between thievery in sex and thievery in gold. Sex and money are both commodities to be protected by watchful fathers against libidinous and opportunistic children.

We as audience make plentiful allowance for Iago's bias in all this, since he has admitted to Roderigo his knavery and resentment of Othello. Even so, the carnal vision of love we confront is calculatedly disturbing, because it seems so equated with a pejorative image of blackness. Othello is unquestionably a black man, referred to disparagingly by his detractors as the "thick-lips," with a "sooty bosom" (1.1.68; 1.2.71); Elizabethan usage applied the term "Moor" to Africans without attempting to distinguish between Arabian and Negroid peoples. From the ugly start of the play, Othello and Desdemona have to prove the worth of their love in the face of preset attitudes against miscegenation. Brabantio takes refuge in the thought that Othello must have bewitched Desdemona. His basic assumption—one to be echoed later by Iago and by Othello himself—is that miscegenation is unnatural by definition. In confronting and accusing Othello he repeatedly appeals "to all things of sense" (that is, to common sense) and asks if it is not "gross in sense" (self-evident) that Othello has practiced magic on her, since nothing else could prompt human nature so to leave its natural path. "For nature so preposterously to err, / Being not deficient, blind, or lame of sense, / Sans witchcraft could not" (1.2.65, 73; 1.3.64–66). We as audience do not endorse Brabantio's view and recognize in him the type of imperious father who conventionally opposes romantic love. It is sadly ironic that he should now prefer Roderigo as a son-in-law, evidently concluding that any white Venetian would be preferable to the prince of blacks. Still, Brabantio has been hospitable to the Moor and trusting of his daughter. He is a sorrowful rather than ridiculous figure, and the charge he levels at the married pair, however much based on a priori assumptions of what is "natural" in human behavior, remains to be answered.

After all, we find ourselves wondering, what did attract Othello and Desdemona to each other? Even though he certainly did not use witchcraft, may Othello not have employed a subtler kind of enchantment in the exotic character of his travels among "the Cannibals that each other eat, / The Anthropophagi, and men whose heads / Do grow beneath their shoulders" (1.3.145–147)? These "passing strange" events fascinate Desdemona as they do everyone including the Duke of Venice ("I think this tale would win my daughter too"). Othello has not practiced unfairly on her—"This only is the witchcraft I have used" (ll. 162, 173, 171). Yet may he not represent for Desdemona a radical novelty, being a man at once less devious and more mysterious than the dissolute Venetian swaggerers such as Roderigo and the "wealthy curlèd darlings of our nation" (1.2.69) who follow her about? Was her deceiving of her father by means of the elopement a protest, an escape from conventionality? Why has she been attracted to a man so much older than herself? For his part, Othello gives the impression of being inexperienced with women, at least of Desdemona's rank and complexion, and is both intrigued and flattered by her attentions. "She loved me for the dangers I had passed, / And I loved her that she did pity them" (1.3.169–170). Desdemona fulfills a place in Othello's view of himself. Does she also represent status for him in Venetian society, where he has been employed as a military commander but treated nonetheless as something of an alien?

These subtle but impertinent ways of doubting the motivations of Othello and Desdemona are thrust upon us by the play's opening and are later crucial to Iago's strategy of breeding mistrust. Just as important, however, these insinuations are refuted by Othello and especially by Desdemona. Whatever others may think, she never gives the slightest indication of regarding her husband as different or exotic because he is black and old. In fact the images of blackness and age are significantly reversed during the play's early scenes. Othello's blackness, like that of the natives dwelling in heathen lands, could betoken to Elizabethan audiences an innocent proneness to accept Christianity, and Othello is one who has already embraced the Christian faith. His first appearance onstage, when he confronts a party of torch-bearing men coming to arrest him and bids his followers sheathe their swords, is sufficiently reminiscent of Christ's arrest in the Garden of Gethsemane to convey a fleeting comparison between Othello and the Christian God whose charity and forbearance he seeks to emulate. Othello's blackness may be used in part as an emblem of fallen man, but so are we all fallen. His age similarly strengthens our impression of his wisdom, restraint, leadership. Any suggestions of comic sexual infidelity in the marriage of an old man and an attractive young bride are confuted by what we see in Desdemona's chaste yet sensual regard for the good man she has chosen.

Desdemona is utterly fond of Othello, admiring, and faithful. We believe her when she says that she does not even know what it means to be unfaithful; the word "whore" is not in her vocabulary. She is defenseless against the charges brought against her because she does not even comprehend them, cannot believe that anyone would imagine such things. Her love, both erotic and chaste, is of that transcendent wholesomeness common to several late Shakespearean heroines such as Cordelia in *King Lear* and Hermione in *The Winter's Tale*. Her "preferring" Othello to her father, like Cordelia's placing her duty to a husband before that to a father, is not ungrateful but natural and proper. And Othello, however much he may regard Desdemona as an extension of himself (he calls her "my fair warrior"), does cherish Desdemona as she deserves. "I cannot speak enough of this content," he exclaims when he rejoins her on Cyprus. "It stops me here; it is too much of joy" (2.1.181, 196–197). The passionate intensity of his love prepares the way for his tragedy, for he knows only too well that "when I love thee not, / Chaos is come again" (3.3.99–100). Iago speaks truly when he observes that Othello "Is of a constant, loving, noble nature" (2.1.290). Othello's tragedy is not that he is easily duped, but that his strong faith can be destroyed at such terrible cost. Othello never forgets how much he is losing. The threat to his love is not an initial lack of wholesomeness, but rather the insidious assumption that Desdemona cannot love him because such a love is unnatural. The fear of being unlovable exists in Othello's mind, but the human instrument of this vicious gospel is Iago.

Iago belongs to a select group of villains in Shakespeare who, while plausibly motivated in human terms, also take delight in evil for its own sake: Aaron the Moor in *Titus Andronicus*, Richard III, Don John in *Much Ado*, Iago, Edmund in *King Lear*. They are not, like Macbeth or like Claudius in *Hamlet*, men driven by ambition to commit crimes they clearly recognize to be wrong. Although Edmund does belatedly try to make amends, these villains are essentially conscienceless, sinister, and amused at their own cunning. They are related to one another by a stage metaphor of personified evil derived from the Vice of the morality play, whose typical role is to win the Mankind figure away from virtue and to corrupt him with worldly enticements. Like that engaging tempter, Shakespeare's villains in these plays take the audience into their confidence, boast in soliloquy of their cleverness, exult in the triumph of evil, and improvise plans with daring and resourcefulness. They are all superb actors, deceiving virtually every character onstage until late in the action with their protean and hypocritical display. They take pleasure in this "sport" and amaze us by their virtuosity. The role is paradoxically comic in its use of ingenious and resourceful deception, although it is the grim and ironic comedy of vice. We know that we are to condemn morally even while we applaud the skill.

The tradition of vice comedy may best explain a puzzling feature of Iago, noted long ago and memorably phrased by Samuel Taylor Coleridge as "the motive-hunting of motiveless malignity." Iago does offer plausible motives for what he does. Despite his resemblance to the morality Vice, he is no allegorized abstraction but an ensign in the army, a junior field officer who hates being outranked by a theoretician or staff officer. As an old-school professional he also resents that he has not been promoted on the basis of seniority, the "old gradation" (1.1.38). Even his efforts at using influence with Othello have come to naught, and Iago can scarcely be blamed for supposing that Cassio's friendship with Othello has won him special favor. Thus Iago has reason to plot against Cassio as well as Othello. Nevertheless a further dimension is needed to explain the gloating, the utter lack of moral reflection, the concentration on destroying Desdemona (who has not wronged Iago), the absorption in ingenious methods of plotting, the finesse and the style. Hatred precedes any plausible motive in Iago, and ultimately does not depend on psychological causality. Probably the tradition of the stage Machiavel (another type of gloating villain based on stereotyped attitudes toward the heretical political ideas of Niccolò Machiavelli), as in

Marlowe's *Jew of Malta*, adds an ingredient; this tradition was readily assimilated with that of the Vice.

Iago's machinations yield him both "sport" and "profit" (1.3.387); that is, he enjoys his evildoing, although he is also driven by a motive. This Vice-like behavior in human garb creates a restless sense of a dark metaphysical reality lying behind his visible exterior. Even his stated motives do not always make sense. When in an outburst of hatred he soliloquizes that "I hate the Moor; / And it is thought abroad that twixt my sheets / He's done my office," Iago goes on to concede the unlikelihood of this charge. "I know not if 't be true; / But I, for mere suspicion in that kind, / Will do as if for surety" (ll. 387–391). The charge is so absurd, in fact, that we have to look into Iago himself for the origin of this jealous paranoia. The answer may be partly emblematic: as the embodiment and genius of sexual jealousy, Iago suffers with ironic appropriateness from the evil he preaches, and without external cause. Emilia understands that jealousy is not a rational affliction but a self-induced disease of the mind. Jealous persons, she tells Desdemona, "are not ever jealous for the cause, / But jealous for they're jealous. It is a monster / Begot upon itself, born on itself" (3.4.161–163). Iago's own testimonial bears this out, for his jealousy is at once wholly irrational and agonizingly self-destructive. "I do suspect the lusty Moor / Hath leaped into my seat, the thought whereof / Doth, like a poisonous mineral, gnaw my innards" (2.1.296–298). In light of this nightmare, we can see that even his seemingly plausible resentment of Cassio's promotion is jealous envy. The "daily beauty" in Cassio's life makes Iago feel "ugly" by comparison (5.1.19–20), engendering in Iago a profound sense of lack of worth from which he can temporarily find relief only by reducing Othello and others to his own miserable condition. He is adept at provoking self-hatred in others because he suffers from it himself.

Othello comes at last to regard Iago as a "demi-devil" who has tempted Othello to damn himself "beneath all depth in hell"; Lodovico speaks of Iago in the closing lines of the play as a "hellish villain" (5.2.309, 142, 379); and Iago himself boasts that "When devils will the blackest sins put on, / They do suggest at first with heavenly shows, / As I do now" (2.3.345–347). Iago thus bears some affinity to both Vice and devil, suggesting his relationship both to Othello's inner temptation and to a preexistent evil force in the universe itself. Conversely, Desdemona is in Emilia's words an "angel," purely chaste, "So come my soul to bliss as I speak true" (5.2.134, 259). When Desdemona lands on Cyprus, she is greeted in words that echo the *Ave Maria:* "Hail to thee, lady! And the grace of heaven . . . Enwheel thee round!" (2.1.87–89). These images introduce metaphorically a conflict of good and evil in which Othello, typical of fallen man, has chosen evil and destroyed the good at the prompting of a diabolical counselor. Again we see the heritage of the morality play, especially of the later morality in which the Mankind figure was sometimes damned rather than saved. Even so, to allegorize *Othello* is to obscure and misread its clash of human passion. In fact, we see that the impulse to reduce human complexity to simplistic moral absolutes is a fatal weakness in Othello; by insisting on viewing Desdemona as a type or abstraction, he loses sight of her wonderful humanity. The theological issue of salvation or damnation is not relevant in dramatic terms; the play is not a homily on the dangers of jealousy. The metaphysical dimensions of a homiletic tradition are transmuted into human drama. Acknowledging these limitations, we can notwithstanding see a spiritual analogy in Iago's devil-like method of undoing his victims.

His trick resembles that of the similarly mischief-making Don John in *Much Ado about Nothing:* an optical illusion by which the blameless heroine is impugned as an adulteress. The concealed Othello must watch Cassio boasting of sexual triumphs and believe he is talking about Desdemona. Like the devil, Iago is given power over men's frail senses, especially the eyes. He can create illusions to induce Othello to see what Iago wants him to see, as Don John does with Claudio, but Othello's acceptance of the lie must be his own responsibility, a failure of his corrupted will. Iago practices on Othello with an a priori logic used before on Brabantio and Roderigo, urging the proneness of all mortals to sin and the unnaturalness of a black-white marriage. All women have appetites; Desdemona is a woman; hence Desdemona has appetites. "The wine she drinks is made of grapes," he scoffs to Roderigo. "If she had been blessed, she would never have loved the Moor" (2.1.253–255). She is a Venetian, and "In Venice they do let God see the pranks / They dare not show their husbands" (3.3.216–217). Therefore she too is a hypocrite; "She did deceive her father" (l. 220). Most of all, it stands to reason that she must long for a man of her own race. As Iago succeeds in getting Othello to ponder: "And yet, how nature erring from itself—" (l. 243). This proposition that Nature teaches all persons, including Desdemona, to seek a harmonious matching of "clime, complexion, and degree" strikes a responsive chord in Othello, since he knows that he is black and alien. "Haply, for I am black / And have not those soft parts of conversation / That chamberers have." Then, too, he is sensitive that he is considerably older than she, "declined / Into the vale of years" (ll. 246, 279–282), "the young affects / In me defunct" (1.3.266–267). And so, if one must conclude from the preceding that Desdemona will seek a lover, the only question is who. "This granted—as it is a most pregnant and unforced position—who stands so eminent in the degree of this fortune as Cassio does?" (2.1.237–239). Once Othello has accepted this syllogistic sequence of proofs, specious not through any lapse in logic but because the axiomatic assumptions about human nature are degraded and do not apply to Desdemona, Othello has arrived at an unshakable conclusion to which all subsequent evidence must be forced as "a foregone conclusion." "Villain, be sure thou prove my love a whore," he commissions Iago (3.3.443, 375). Desdemona's innocent pleading for Cassio only makes things look worse. Cassio's reputed muttering while asleep, like the handkerchief seen in his possession or his giddy talk about his mistress Bianca, "speaks against her [Desdemona] with the other proofs" (l. 456).

How has Othello fallen so far in so short a time? His bliss with Desdemona as they are reunited on Cyprus knows no limit. These two persons represent married love at its very best, erotic and spiritual, she enhancing his manliness, he cherishing her beauty and virtue. His blackness and age are positive images in him, despite earlier insinuations to the contrary. He is a man of public worthiness, of command, of self-assurance. Desdemona is the most domestic of Shakespeare's tragic heroines, even while she is also representative of so much that is transcendent. Husband and wife are bound happily in one of Shakespeare's few detailed portraits of serious commitment in marriage. What then gives way? We look at Iago for one important insight, but ultimately the cause must be in Othello himself. Arthur Kirsch has argued persuasively (in *Shakespeare and the Experience of Love*, 1981) that Othello's most grave failing is an insufficient regard for himself. It is in part an inability to counter the effects on him of a culture that regards him as an outsider; he is at last persuaded to see himself with the eyes of Venice, not just of Iago but of Brabantio (who gladly entertains Othello until he has the presumption to elope with Brabantio's white daughter) and others. The resulting destruction of self-regard is devastating. Othello's jealousy stems from a profound suspicion that others cannot love him because he does not deem himself lovable.

Othello has loved Desdemona as an extension of himself, and in his moments of greatest contentedness his marriage is sustained by an idealized vision of Desdemona serving as the object of his exalted romantic passion. When he destroys Desdemona, as he realizes with a terrible clarity, Othello destroys himself; the act is a prelude to his actual suicide. Iago's mode of temptation, then, is to persuade Othello to regard himself with the eyes of Venice, to accept the view that Othello is himself alien and that any woman who loves him does so perversely. In Othello's tainted state of mind, Desdemona's very sexuality becomes an unbearable threat to him, her warmth and devotion a "proof" of disloyalty. Othello's most tortured speeches (3.4.57–77, 4.2.49–66) reveal the extent to which he equates the seemingly betraying woman he has so depended on for happiness with his own mother, who gave Othello's father a handkerchief and threatened him with loss of her love if he should lose it. Othello has briefly learned and then forgotten the precious art of harmonizing erotic passion and spiritual love, and as these two great aims of love are driven apart in him, he comes to loathe and fear the sexuality that puts him so much in mind of his physical frailty and dependence on woman. The horror and pity of *Othello* rests above all in the spectacle of a love that was once so whole and noble made filthy by self-hatred.

The increasing surrender of Othello's judgment to passion can be measured in three successive trial scenes in the play: the entirely fair trial of Othello himself by the Venetian senate concerning the elopement, Othello's trial of Cassio for drinking and rioting (when, ominously, Othello's "blood begins my safer guides to rule"; 2.3.199), and finally the prejudged sentencing of Desdemona without any opportunity for her to defend herself. In a corollary decline, Othello falls from the Christian compassion of the opening scenes (he customarily confesses to heaven "the vices of my blood," 1.3.125) to the pagan savagery of his vengeful and ritualistic execution of his wife. "My heart is turned to stone" (4.1.182–183), he vows, and at the play's end he grievingly characterizes himself as a "base Indian" who "threw a pearl away / Richer than all his tribe" (5.2.357–358). (The First Folio reading of "Iudean" or "Judean" refers perhaps to Judas Iscariot or to Herod; most editors prefer the quarto reading of "Indian.") Iago knows that he must persuade Othello to sentence and execute Desdemona himself, for only by active commitment to evil will Othello damn himself. In nothing does Iago so resemble the devil as in his wish to see Othello destroy the innocence and goodness on which his happiness depends.

The fate of some of the lesser characters echoes that of Othello, for Iago's evil intent is to "enmesh them all" (2.3.356). Cassio in particular is, like Othello, an attractive man with a single but fatally vulnerable weakness, in his case a fleshly appetite for wine and women. For him, alternately idolizing and depreciating women as he does, the gap between spiritual and sensual love remains vast, but he is essentially good-natured and trustworthy. His seemingly genial flaws lead to disaster because they put him at the mercy of a remorseless enemy. Iago is, with fitting irony, the apostle of absolute self-control: "Our bodies are our gardens, to the which our wills are gardeners" (1.3.323–324). Thus, Cassio's tragedy is anything but a straightforward homily on the virtues of temperance. Similarly, Bianca is undone not through any simple cause-and-effect punishment of her sexual conduct—she is, after all, fond of Cassio and loyal to him, even if he will not marry her—but because Iago is able to turn appearances against

her. With his usual appeal to a priori logic, he builds a case
that she and Cassio are in cahoots: "I do suspect this trash /
To be a party in this injury. . . . This is the fruits of whoring"
(5.1.86–87, 118). Roderigo is another of Iago's victims, a
contemptible one, led by the nose because he too has sur-
rendered reason to passion. Emilia cannot escape Iago's
evil influence and gives the handkerchief to him despite
knowing its value for Desdemona. Flaws are magnified into
disasters by a remorseless evil intelligence. Men must be
ceaselessly circumspect; a good reputation is sooner lost
than recovered. Emilia is a conventionally decent enough
woman—she would be faithless in marriage, she tells Desdemona, only for a very high price—and yet her one small
compromise with her conscience contributes to the murder
of her mistress. Like Othello she offers atonement too late,
by denouncing her husband. Desdemona is the only person
in the play too good to be struck down through some inner
flaw, which may explain why Iago is committed above all
else to seeing that she be destroyed.

As a tragic hero, Othello obtains self-knowledge at a terrible price. He knows finally that what he has destroyed was
ineffably good. The discovery is too late for him to make
amends, and he dies by his own hand as atonement. The
deaths of Othello and Desdemona are, in their separate
ways, equally devastating: he is in part the victim of racism,
though he nobly refuses to deny his own culpability, and
she is the victim of sexism, lapsing sadly into the stereo-
typical role of passive and silent sufferer that has been
demanded of her. Despite the loss, however, Othello's re-
affirmation of faith in Desdemona's goodness undoes what
the devil-like Iago had most hoped to achieve: the separation of Othello from a belief in goodness. In this important
sense, Othello's self-knowledge is cathartic and a compen-
sation for the terrible price he has paid. The very existence
of a person as good as Desdemona gives the lie to Iago's
creed that everyone has his or her price. She is the sacrifi-
cial victim who must die for Othello's loss of faith and, by
dying, rekindle that faith. ("My life upon her faith!" Othello
prophetically affirms, in response to her father's warning
that she may deceive him [1.3.297].) She cannot restore him
to himself, for self-hatred has done its ugly work, but she is

the means by which he understands at last the chimerical
and wantonly destructive nature of his jealousy. His great-
ness appears in his acknowledgment of this truth, and in
the heroic struggle with which he has confronted an inner
darkness we all share.

Othello
in Performance

To a remarkable extent, the history of *Othello* in performance is the history of lead actors in the roles of Othello and Iago. Desdemona occasionally captures attention, sometimes even Cassio, but the rest of the play is largely forgotten. Scenic effects are not essential. Props are at a minimum. Indeed, there are only thirteen speaking parts. The play onstage depends almost entirely on the personal magnetism of the leading player and one or two others. Small wonder that Othello's role has been coveted by most of the famous actors in every age.

Richard Burbage played Othello in Shakespeare's company, regularly at the Globe Theatre, and at court in 1604 and again in 1613. An elegy written upon Burbage's death in 1619 remembers his "grieved Moor" among his great roles. Thomas Killigrew, who obtained the rights to *Othello* after the Restoration, performed the play with his King's men at the Cockpit. Samuel Pepys saw this production on October 11, 1660, remarking in his diary: "a pretty lady that sat by me called out to see Desdemona smothered." Thomas Betterton played Othello with great intensity from 1683 to 1709, primarily after 1703 at the theater in Lincoln's Inn Fields, London. One contemporary witness testified that "his aspect was serious, venerable, and majestic." Barton Booth, James Quin, and Spranger Barry were the great Othellos after Betterton on the Restoration and eighteenth-century stage. Oddly, David Garrick was not successful in the role: he acted Othello in two seasons only, abandoning the part for Iago in 1746. Garrick's small, wiry body and his nervous emotional intensity did not match the age's preference for a heroic protagonist. John Philip Kemble first played Othello in 1785 and struggled through various productions until 1805, but had no better luck. Kemble failed because of what his biographer James Boaden has called the "philosophy in his bearing and reason in his rage." Audiences seemed to demand from Othello either the towering violent jealousy projected by Betterton or the grandeur and presence of Quin. Spranger Barry, combining something of both, was the most successful Othello of the century, fierce in his rage but so poignant in his grief that, as a reviewer noted, "the audience seemed to lose the energies of their hands, and could only thank him with their tears." Iago, played by Lacy Ryan, Colley Cibber, and Charles Macklin, among others, required melodramatic villainy, though Macklin also provided some real depth of characterization, naturalizing his performance so that (in Macklin's words) Iago's "seeming openness and concealed revenge" became a plausible, if terrifying, human response to the goodness surrounding him. Anne Bracegirdle and Susannah Cibber were the outstanding Desdemonas of the age, energetically asserting their innocence. The play was enormously popular throughout the period, no doubt because of the persuasive acting of its principals. It was staged in all but seven years of the entire eighteenth century.

The play was cut to center attention on its main figures and to enhance the tragic nobility of the protagonist. Bell's acting version of 1773 is representative of the tradition. It omits Othello's mention of anthropophagi, cannibals, and "antres vast," does away with the storm scene for the landing in Cyprus in Act 2, cuts the Clown scene (3.1) in the interests of classical unity and decorum, banishes Bianca for reasons of moral decency, takes away the scene in which Othello's jealousy is confirmed by seeing the handkerchief in Cassio's hand, and deprives Desdemona of her conversation with Emilia before her death. The death itself is accomplished by stabbing. What remains in the text is chiefly a series of lofty tragic scenes for Othello and Iago.

Othello in the nineteenth century belonged for the most part to Edmund Kean, Edwin Booth, and Tommaso Salvini; Samuel Phelps also succeeded in the role. Kean's Othello was the most celebrated, described by critic William Hazlitt as "the finest piece of acting in the world." Kean's appalling fury and final desolation moved audiences to tears. Booth describes his father as believing that "no mortal man could equal Kean in the rendering of Othello's despair and rage." Booth himself was a more noble and humane Othello, as in his production at Booth's Theatre in New York in 1869, but was perhaps more arresting in his portrayal of a gloating and demonic Iago, as at the Winter Garden Theatre in 1866. In 1881, Booth and Henry Irving appeared at London's Lyceum Theatre, alternating the roles of Othello and Iago, with Ellen Terry as Desdemona. The production was a great success, artistically and financially. Irving had played Othello only once before, in 1876, to little acclaim, and he had never played Iago. Still, he was the greatest English actor of his generation, and people flocked to see the collision of titans from England and America. As Othello, Irving could not match the power of Booth's brooding Moor. Irving's Iago, on the other hand, was more than a match for his rival, believably genial in public and savagely sardonic when alone. Yet Irving's success with Iago was not enough to compensate him for being overpowered in the role of Othello. Although the English critics applauded Irving, the measure of Booth's triumph is that Irving never again acted either part. The Italian actor Tommaso Salvini first appeared as Othello in New York at the Academy of Music in 1873 and two years later in London at the Theatre Royal, Drury Lane. His was a fiery, sensual Moor, powerful and dangerous. The theater critic William Winter, disgusted by Salvini's barbaric Othello, claimed that "only because of the excitement that it diffused throughout the nervous systems of the multitude, it possesses a worldwide renown." What Winter intended as a slight seems high praise indeed today.

Though William Charles Macready acted the part often in his career, first in 1814, he felt that he never achieved "the real pathos and terrible fury which belong to the character." Still, his Othello was powerful and dignified, and, in keeping with the attention to realistic detail for which Macready was famous, always correctly attired as a sixteenth-century Venetian officer. When, in 1816, Macready and Charles Mayne Young alternated in the two leading parts, Macready achieved greater success as Iago. Hazlitt remembered Young's Othello as "a great humming-top, and Macready, in Iago, like a mischievous boy whipping him." Samuel Phelps and Charles Fechter also acted Othello with something like Macready's dignity and restraint. Phelps alternated with Macready in the parts of Iago and Othello in 1839 at the Haymarket Theatre, with Helen Faucit as Desdemona. Once again, Macready achieved success with his

Iago, but Phelps's unfussy, gentle Othello, much to Macready's discomfort, carried the day. The *Weekly Dispatch* delightedly remarked: "He was of all things that which we have never witnessed since the death of Kean—natural." The *Sunbeam* proclaimed, even more enthusiastically, "we are now convinced that the Othello of Mr. Phelps is the Othello of Shakespeare." His productions at the Sadler's Wells Theatre, in fifteen of his eighteen years as manager, were great successes, and he continued alternating in the two male leads in seasons when he had another actor capable of performing both. Charles Fechter's Othello was more sentimental than Phelps's, intelligent and affectionate, perhaps better suited, as the *Morning Advertiser* put it, to be the hero of a "French melodrama" than of Shakespeare's agonizing tragedy.

In some remarkable way, the emotional intensity demanded in the playing of *Othello* seemed to encourage actors to carry their theatrical roles over into their private lives. Kean was correspondent in a notorious divorce trial in 1825. In 1833 Kean collapsed into the arms of his son Charles during a performance of *Othello* and died shortly thereafter. The American actor Edwin Forrest brought to his performance of Othello the experience of divorcing his wife for adultery only to be found guilty himself and ordered to pay alimony. Court appeals dragged on for years, leaving Forrest embittered and alienated. The nineteenth-century American black actor Ira Aldridge, who successfully played Othello and other tragic parts in Europe for four decades before his death in 1867, was married to a white woman. Stories such as these, at any rate, fed a popular conception of *Othello* as a shocking and sensational affair, one well suited to the savage fury and sensuality of Salvini's performance. The scene of Desdemona's murder in Salvini's rendition was especially violent, and the production took London by storm. The famous actresses of the age—Sarah Siddons, Anna Mowatt, most of all Ellen Terry—captured the sympathies of audiences by playing to the full the melodramatic role of womanly innocence traduced and overwhelmed.

Sensationalism of this kind is made for opera, and it is no coincidence that the *Othello* of the nineteenth-century stage gave rise to immortal operatic rendition. Gioachino

Rossini's *Otello* (1816) departs too widely from Shakespeare's text to allow meaningful comparison (he relied on Cinthio's story), but Giuseppe Verdi's great *Otello* (1887), the libretto by Arrigo Boito, is integrally a part of the stage history of Shakespeare's play. The omission of the first act in Venice, the concentration on the roles of Otello, Iago, and Desdemona, the ending with Otello's last kiss of his dead wife—all are comparable to those means used by actor-managers to focus the play on the intensely emotional confrontations of the tragic protagonists. Verdi eloquently interpreted the play as it was understood by his generation, and did so with such power that his operatic version remains a central formative influence in today's theater.

The twentieth century has not brought with it a major revision in the staging of *Othello*, in part perhaps because the play does not lend itself to topical appropriation as with the antiwar satire often applied to Shakespeare's histories or the disillusioning view of sex and politics often seen in productions of *Troilus and Cressida* or *Hamlet*. *Othello* does not easily adapt itself to Edwardian decor or the American frontier West, as in some productions of *All's Well That Ends Well* or *Much Ado about Nothing*. In most twentieth-century productions the text is more nearly restored to the original than in those of the previous century, and the balance of parts gives new visibility to Roderigo, Brabantio, Emilia, and Bianca, but the text was never as rearranged as it was for many other plays. Because *Othello* is a play written around a few major roles, the nineteenth century did not have to change a great deal to get what it wanted from this play.

Changes in perception of *Othello* in the twentieth century have accordingly focused on a few delicate and critical issues, most notably that of the relations of the races. For Paul Robeson, a black American actor, the central issue was not sexual jealousy but the granting of human dignity to blacks. Starring in a production with Peggy Ashcroft as Desdemona, Sybil Thorndike as Emilia, and Ralph Richardson as Roderigo at London's Savoy Theatre in 1930, Robeson brought together his personal convictions and professional ambitions in a way very different from that of Kean or Forrest. Earlier actors of Othello, excepting Ira Aldridge, had been whites who could choose to portray a black Othello or a more Arabian and Moorish Othello to suit their own acting styles. Robeson was black, a large man, sonorous of voice, commanding, magisterial. He was also a believer in a cause, and, although limited theatrically to this one role in which he must show violence and loss of emotional control (prejudices of the time did not permit him to play Iago as Booth, Kean, and Phelps had done), the very fact of his sharing the spotlight with Peggy Ashcroft (and later in 1943 with Jose Ferrer and Uta Hagen in Margaret Webster's production at the Shubert Theatre in New York) was in itself significant. He was a man of memorable dignity and presence, and his work opened the way for other blacks, especially Earle Hyman (New York, Jan Hus Auditorium, 1953, and Stratford, Connecticut, 1957), Moses Gunn (Stratford, Connecticut, 1970), and James Earl Jones (New York Shakespeare Festival, 1964, and Stratford, Connecticut, 1981), to succeed in the part. Robeson became a controversial figure and something of an outcast, whereas, when Jones played opposite Christopher Plummer in 1981 at Stratford, Connecticut (a production that in February of 1982 opened at New York's Winter Garden Theatre), his race no longer occasioned comment; Jones had by then already won considerable praise for his portrayal of King Lear.

Today, the role of Othello is available to any leading player, and has been acted by Ralph Richardson in Tyrone Guthrie's production at the Old Vic in 1938, with Laurence Olivier as Iago; by Richard Burton, again at the Old Vic, in 1956, alternating with John Neville in the parts of Othello and Iago; by Emrys James at Stratford-upon-Avon in 1971; by Raul Julia, as a passionate, tortured Othello in Wilford Leach's production for the New York Shakespeare Festival in 1979; by Anthony Hopkins, opposite Bob Hoskins's Iago, in Jonathan Miller's BBC television version in 1981; and by Ben Kingsley, who powerfully revealed the violence at the center of Othello's achieved calm, at Stratford-upon-Avon in 1985. Laurence Olivier played Othello with great success at the Old Vic for the newly established National Theatre in 1964, although he was less convincing in his film version of the production the next year, perhaps because the close-ups made too much of Oliver's West Indian mannerisms and appearance. With his virtuoso performance of an Othello both proud and self-dramatizing, Olivier demonstrated at least that the play remains what it always has been, the vehicle for an astonishing display of acting ability by one of the great actors of the age.

When we locate *Othello* on the Elizabethan stage, we see that the absence of scenery accentuates the focus on character; indeed, scenic effects have seldom played a big part in productions of this play. The Elizabethan actor needs to build the scene around him by his commanding presence and the magic of his words. Costuming and spatial arrangement are also important: in Act 1, scene 1, we know in the Elizabethan theater that we are before Brabantio's house when Desdemona's father appears in the gallery above, at his window, and then reemerges below in his nightgown *"with servants and torches."* Torches are repeatedly necessary in *Othello*, not to illuminate the stage but to signal nighttime. Theatrical signs of darkness are often intensified by violent action, as in the drinking on watch (2.3) or the killing of Roderigo and the wounding of Cassio (5.1). The latter scene, particularly, reveals how actors on the bare Elizabethan stage, in full daylight, convey a sense of darkness and dread: they grope about, look apprehensive, call for lights, and gradually come to understand what the audience, in its omniscience, has known all along.

Illusion-making of this sort is central to a play that is so concerned with deceptive appearances and overhearing. Iago is the master of illusion, and his dominance as a baleful kind of dramatist indicates how hard it is not to be deceived by show. We watch Roderigo, Othello, and indeed virtually everyone fall under the influence of his image-making ability. What are we as audience to believe? We are left in Act 5 with a stage image that focuses our attention on this problem of truth and reputation: Desdemona's bed. Thrust onstage or set in the discovery space at the rear of the stage for the play's final scene, it is a central stage property that tests the very nature of theatrical illusion. Desdemona lies slain within its bed curtains, while Emilia and others struggle to discover what has occurred. Othello, who has begun the scene believing he could snuff out the life of Desdemona as simply as snuffing out a candle, learns too late that Desdemona is not what he, in his diseased imagination, has pictured her to be. The final "tragic loading of this bed" leaves us with an unforgettable picture of Othello's failure, but also of the innocence that his doubt and Iago's slander cannot finally unsay.

The Playhouse

This early copy of a drawing by Johannes de Witt of the Swan Theatre in London (c. 1596), made by his friend Arend van Buchell, is the only surviving contemporary sketch of the interior of a public theater in the 1590s.

From other contemporary evidence, including the stage directions and dialogue of Elizabethan plays, we can surmise that the various public theaters where Shakespeare's plays were produced (the Theatre, the Curtain, the Globe) resembled the Swan in many important particulars, though there must have been some variations as well. The public playhouses were essentially round, or polygonal, and open to the sky, forming an acting arena approximately 70 feet in diameter; they did not have a large curtain with which to open and close a scene, such as we see today in opera and some traditional theater. A platform measuring approximately 43 feet across and 27 feet deep, referred to in the de Witt drawing as the *proscaenium*, projected into the yard, *planities sive arena*. The roof, *tectum*, above the stage and supported by two pillars, could contain machinery for ascents and descents, as were required in several of Shakespeare's late plays. Above this roof was a hut, shown in the drawing with a flag flying atop it and a trumpeter at its door announcing the performance of a play. The underside of the stage roof, called the heavens, was usually richly decorated with symbolic figures of the sun, the moon, and the constellations. The platform stage stood at a height of $5\frac{1}{2}$ feet or so above the yard, providing room under the stage for underworldly effects. A trapdoor, which is not visible in this drawing, gave access to the space below.

The structure at the back of the platform (labeled *mimorum aedes*), known as the tiring-house because it was the actors' attiring (dressing) space, featured at least two doors, as shown here. Some theaters seem to have also had a discovery space, or curtained recessed alcove, perhaps between the two doors—in which Falstaff could have hidden from the sheriff (*1 Henry IV*, 2.4) or Polonius could have eavesdropped on Hamlet and his mother (*Hamlet*, 3.4). This discovery space probably gave the actors a means of access to and from the tiring-house. Curtains may also have been hung in front of the stage doors on occasion. The de Witt drawing shows a gallery above the doors that extends across the back and evidently contains spectators. On occasions when action "above" demanded the use of this space, as when Juliet appears at her "window" (*Romeo and Juliet*, 2.2 and 3.5), the gallery seems to have been used by the actors, but large scenes there were impractical.

The three-tiered auditorium is perhaps best described by Thomas Platter, a visitor to London in 1599 who saw on that occasion Shakespeare's *Julius Caesar* performed at the Globe:

The playhouses are so constructed that they play on a raised platform, so that everyone has a good view. There are different galleries and places [*orchestra, sedilia, porticus*], however, where the seating is better and more comfortable and therefore more expensive. For whoever cares to stand below only pays one English penny, but if he wishes to sit, he enters by another door [*ingressus*] and pays another penny, while if he desires to sit in the most comfortable seats, which are cushioned, where he not only sees everything well but can also be seen, then he pays yet another English penny at another door. And during the performance food and drink are carried round the audience, so that for what one cares to pay one may also have refreshment.

Scenery was not used, though the theater building itself was handsome enough to invoke a feeling of order and hierarchy that lent itself to the splendor and pageantry onstage. Portable properties, such as thrones, stools, tables, and beds, could be carried or thrust on as needed. In the scene pictured here by de Witt, a lady on a bench, attended perhaps by her waiting-gentlewoman, receives the address of a male figure. If Shakespeare had written *Twelfth Night* by 1596 for performance at the Swan, we could imagine Malvolio appearing like this as he bows before the Countess Olivia and her gentlewoman, Maria.

OTHELLO

The Names of the Actors

OTHELLO, *the Moor*
BRABANTIO, [*a senator,*] *father to Desdemona*
CASSIO, *an honorable lieutenant* [*to Othello*]
IAGO, [*Othello's ancient,*] *a villain*
RODERIGO, *a gulled gentleman*
DUKE OF VENICE
SENATORS [*of Venice*]
MONTANO, *Governor of Cyprus*
GENTLEMEN *of Cyprus*
LODOVICO *and* GRATIANO, [*kinsmen to Brabantio,*] *two noble*
    Venetians
SAILORS
CLOWN

DESDEMONA, [*daughter to Brabantio and*] *wife to Othello*
EMILIA, *wife to Iago*
BIANCA, *a courtesan* [*and mistress to Cassio*]

[A MESSENGER
A HERALD
A MUSICIAN

Servants, Attendants, Officers, Senators, Musicians, Gentlemen

SCENE: *Venice; a seaport in Cyprus*]

1.1   *Enter Roderigo and Iago.*

RODERIGO
  Tush, never tell me! I take it much unkindly   1
  That thou, Iago, who hast had my purse
  As if the strings were thine, shouldst know of this.   ·3
IAGO 'Sblood, but you'll not hear me.   4
  If ever I did dream of such a matter,
  Abhor me.
RODERIGO
  Thou toldst me thou didst hold him in thy hate.
IAGO Despise me
  If I do not. Three great ones of the city,
  In personal suit to make me his lieutenant,
  Off-capped to him; and by the faith of man,   11
  I know my price, I am worth no worse a place.
  But he, as loving his own pride and purposes,
  Evades them with a bombast circumstance   14
  Horribly stuffed with epithets of war,   15
  And, in conclusion,
  Nonsuits my mediators. For, "Certes," says he,   17
  "I have already chose my officer."
  And what was he?
  Forsooth, a great arithmetician,   20
  One Michael Cassio, a Florentine,
  A fellow almost damned in a fair wife,   22
  That never set a squadron in the field
  Nor the division of a battle knows   24
  More than a spinster—unless the bookish theoric,   25
  Wherein the togaed consuls can propose   26
  As masterly as he. Mere prattle without practice

1.1. Location: Venice. A street.
1 never tell me don't talk to me **3 this** i.e., Desdemona's elopement
4 'Sblood by His (Christ's) blood **11 him** i.e., Othello **14 bombast
circumstance** wordy evasion. (*Bombast* is cotton padding.) **15 epithets
of war** military expressions **17 Nonsuits** rejects the petition of. **Certes**
certainly **20 arithmetician** i.e., a man whose military knowledge is
merely theoretical, based on books of tactics **22 A . . . wife** (Cassio
does not seem to be married, but his counterpart in Shakespeare's
source does have a woman in his house. See also 4.1.131.) **24 division
of a battle** disposition of a military unit **25 a spinster** i.e., a housewife,
one whose regular occupation is spinning. **theoric** theory **26 togaed**
wearing the toga. **consuls** counselors, senators. **propose** discuss

Is all his soldiership. But he, sir, had th' election;
And I, of whom his eyes had seen the proof   29
At Rhodes, at Cyprus, and on other grounds
Christened and heathen, must be beleed and calmed   31
By debitor and creditor. This countercaster,   32
He, in good time, must his lieutenant be,   33
And I—God bless the mark!—his Moorship's ancient.   34

RODERIGO
By heaven, I rather would have been his hangman.   35

IAGO
Why, there's no remedy. 'Tis the curse of service;
Preferment goes by letter and affection,   37
And not by old gradation, where each second   38
Stood heir to the first. Now, sir, be judge yourself
Whether I in any just term am affined   40
To love the Moor.

RODERIGO   I would not follow him, then.

IAGO   O sir, content you.   43
I follow him to serve my turn upon him.
We cannot all be masters, nor all masters
Cannot be truly followed. You shall mark   46
Many a duteous and knee-crooking knave
That, doting on his own obsequious bondage,
Wears out his time, much like his master's ass,
For naught but provender, and when he's old, cashiered.   50
Whip me such honest knaves. Others there are   51
Who, trimmed in forms and visages of duty,   52
Keep yet their hearts attending on themselves,
And, throwing but shows of service on their lords,

---

29 his i.e., Othello's   **31 Christened** i.e., Christian. **beleed and calmed**
left to leeward without wind, becalmed. (A sailing metaphor.)
32 debitor and creditor (A name for a system of bookkeeping, here used
as a contemptuous nickname for Cassio.) **countercaster** i.e., book-
keeper, one who tallies with *counters* or metal disks. (Said contemptu-
ously.)   **33 in good time** i.e., forsooth   **34 God bless the mark** (Perhaps
originally a formula to ward off evil; here an expression of impatience.)   **ancient** standard-bearer, ensign   **35 his hangman** the execu-
tioner of him   **37 Preferment** promotion. **letter and affection** personal
influence and favoritism   **38 old gradation** step-by-step seniority, the
traditional way   **40 term** respect. **affined** bound   **43 content you** don't
you worry about that   **46 truly** faithfully   **50 cashiered** dismissed from
service   **51 Whip me** whip, as far as I'm concerned   **52 trimmed . . .
duty** dressed up in the mere form and show of dutifulness

Do well thrive by them, and when they have lined their
  coats,   55
Do themselves homage. These fellows have some soul, 56
And such a one do I profess myself. For, sir,
It is as sure as you are Roderigo,
Were I the Moor I would not be Iago.   59
In following him, I follow but myself—
Heaven is my judge, not I for love and duty,
But seeming so for my peculiar end.   62
For when my outward action doth demonstrate
The native act and figure of my heart   64
In compliment extern, 'tis not long after   65
But I will wear my heart upon my sleeve .
For daws to peck at. I am not what I am.   67

RODERIGO
What a full fortune does the thick lips owe   68
If he can carry 't thus!
IAGO   Call up her father.   69
Rouse him, make after him, poison his delight,
Proclaim him in the streets; incense her kinsmen,
And, though he in a fertile climate dwell,   72
Plague him with flies. Though that his joy be joy, 73
Yet throw such changes of vexation on 't   74
As it may lose some color.   75

RODERIGO
Here is her father's house. I'll call aloud.
IAGO
Do, with like timorous accent and dire yell   77

---

55 lined their coats i.e., stuffed their purses **56 Do themselves homage**
i.e., attend to self-interest solely **59 Were . . . Iago** i.e., if I were able to
assume command I certainly would not choose to remain a subordi-
nate **62 peculiar** particular, personal **64 native** innate. **figure** shape,
intent **65 compliment extern** outward show (conforming in this case to
the inner workings and intention of the heart) **67 I am not what I am**
i.e., I am not one who wears his heart on his sleeve **68 full** swelling.
thick-lips (Elizabethans often applied the term "Moor" to Negroes.)
owe own **69 carry 't thus** carry this off **72–73 though . . . flies** i.e.,
though he seems prosperous and happy now, vex him with misery
73 Though . . . be joy i.e., although he seems fortunate and happy.
(Repeats the idea of l. 72.) **74 changes of vexation** vexing changes
75 As it may that may cause it to. **some color** i.e., some of its fresh
gloss **77 timorous** frightening

As when, by night and negligence, the fire   78
Is spied in populous cities.

RODERIGO
What ho, Brabantio! Signor Brabantio, ho!

IAGO
Awake! What ho, Brabantio! Thieves, thieves, thieves!
Look to your house, your daughter, and your bags!
Thieves, thieves!   83

   Brabantio [enters] above [at a window].

BRABANTIO
What is the reason of this terrible summons?
What is the matter there?   85

RODERIGO
Signor, is all your family within?

IAGO
Are your doors locked?

BRABANTIO   Why, wherefore ask you this?

IAGO
Zounds, sir, you're robbed. For shame, put on your
   gown!   88
Your heart is burst; you have lost half your soul.
Even now, now, very now, an old black ram
Is tupping your white ewe. Arise, arise!   91
Awake the snorting citizens with the bell,   92
Or else the devil will make a grandsire of you.   93
Arise, I say!

BRABANTIO   What, have you lost your wits?

RODERIGO
Most reverend signor, do you know my voice?

BRABANTIO   Not I. What are you?

RODERIGO   My name is Roderigo.

BRABANTIO   The worser welcome.
I have charged thee not to haunt about my doors.
In honest plainness thou hast heard me say
My daughter is not for thee; and now, in madness,

---

78 and negligence i.e., caused by negligence   **83 s.d. at a window** (This
stage direction, from the quarto, probably calls for an appearance on
the gallery above and rearstage.)   **85 the matter** your business
88 Zounds by His (Christ's) wounds   **91 tupping** covering, copulating
with. (Said of sheep.)   **92 snorting** snoring   **93 the devil** (The devil was
conventionally pictured as black.)

Being full of supper and distempering drafts,   102
Upon malicious bravery dost thou come   103
To start my quiet.   104

RODERIGO
Sir, sir, sir—

BRABANTIO   But thou must needs be sure
My spirits and my place have in their power   106
To make this bitter to thee.

RODERIGO   Patience, good sir.

BRABANTIO
What tell'st thou me of robbing? This is Venice;
My house is not a grange.

RODERIGO   Most grave Brabantio,   109
In simple and pure soul I come to you.   110

IAGO Zounds, sir, you are one of those that will not
serve God if the devil bid you. Because we come to do
you service and you think we are ruffians, you'll have
your daughter covered with a Barbary horse; you'll
have your nephews neigh to you; you'll have coursers   115
for cousins and jennets for germans.   116

BRABANTIO What profane wretch art thou?

IAGO I am one, sir, that comes to tell you your daughter
and the Moor are now making the beast with two
backs.

BRABANTIO
Thou art a villain.

IAGO   You are—a senator.

BRABANTIO
This thou shalt answer. I know thee, Roderigo.   122

RODERIGO
Sir, I will answer anything. But, I beseech you,
If 't be your pleasure and most wise consent—
As partly I find it is—that your fair daughter,
At this odd-even and dull watch o' the night,   126

---

102 distempering intoxicating **103 Upon malicious bravery** with hostile intent to defy me **104 start** startle, disrupt **106 My spirits and my place** my temperament and my authority of office. **have in** have it in **109 grange** isolated farmhouse **110 simple** sincere **115 nephews** i.e., grandsons. **coursers** powerful horses **116 cousins** kinsmen. **jennets** small Spanish horses. **germans** near relatives **122 answer** be held accountable for **126 odd-even** between one day and the next, i.e., about midnight

Transported with no worse nor better guard   127
But with a knave of common hire, a gondolier,   128
To the gross clasps of a lascivious Moor—
If this be known to you and your allowance   130
We then have done you bold and saucy wrongs.   131
But if you know not this, my manners tell me
We have your wrong rebuke. Do not believe
That, from the sense of all civility,   134
I thus would play and trifle with your reverence.   135
Your daughter, if you have not given her leave,
I say again, hath made a gross revolt,
Tying her duty, beauty, wit, and fortunes   138
In an extravagant and wheeling stranger   139
Of here and everywhere. Straight satisfy yourself.   140
If she be in her chamber or your house,
Let loose on me the justice of the state
For thus deluding you.
BRABANTIO   Strike on the tinder, ho!   144
    Give me a taper! Call up all my people!
    This accident is not unlike my dream.   146
    Belief of it oppresses me already.
    Light, I say, light!   *Exit [above]*.
IAGO   Farewell, for I must leave you.
    It seems not meet nor wholesome to my place
    To be producted—as, if I stay, I shall—   150
    Against the Moor. For I do know the state,
    However this may gall him with some check,   152
    Cannot with safety cast him, for he's embarked   153
    With such loud reason to the Cyprus wars,   154
    Which even now stands in act, that, for their souls,   155
    Another of his fathom they have none   156

---

127 with by   **128 But with a knave** than by a low fellow, a servant
130 allowance permission   **131 saucy** insolent   **134 from** contrary to.
civility good manners, decency   **135 your reverence** the respect due to
you   **138 wit** intelligence   **139 extravagant** expatriate, wandering far
from home.   **wheeling** roving about, vagabond.   **stranger** foreigner
140 Straight straightway   **144 tinder** charred linen ignited by a spark
from flint and steel, used to light torches or *tapers* (ll. 145, 170)
146 accident occurrence, event   **150 producted** produced (as a witness)   **152 gall** rub; oppress.   **check** rebuke   **153 cast** dismiss.   **em-
barked** engaged   **154 loud** i.e., self-evident, boldly proclaimed
155 stands in act are going on   **156 fathom** i.e., ability, depth of
experience

To lead their business; in which regard,   157
Though I do hate him as I do hell pains,
Yet for necessity of present life   159
I must show out a flag and sign of love,
Which is indeed but sign. That you shall surely find him,
Lead to the Sagittary the raisèd search,   162
And there will I be with him. So farewell.   *Exit.* 163

    Enter [below] Brabantio [in his nightgown] with
    servants and torches.

BRABANTIO
It is too true an evil. Gone she is;
And what's to come of my despisèd time   165
Is naught but bitterness. Now, Roderigo,
Where didst thou see her?—O unhappy girl!—
With the Moor, sayst thou?—Who would be a father!—
How didst thou know 'twas she?—O, she deceives me
Past thought!—What said she to you?—Get more tapers.
Raise all my kindred.—Are they married, think you?

RODERIGO Truly, I think they are.

BRABANTIO
O heaven! How got she out? O treason of the blood!
Fathers, from hence trust not your daughters' minds
By what you see them act. Is there not charms   175
By which the property of youth and maidhood   176
May be abused? Have you not read, Roderigo,   177
Of some such thing?

RODERIGO   Yes, sir, I have indeed.

BRABANTIO
Call up my brother.—O, would you had had her!—
Some one way, some another.—Do you know
Where we may apprehend her and the Moor?

RODERIGO
I think I can discover him, if you please   182
To get good guard and go along with me.

---

157 in which regard out of regard for which   **159 life** livelihood
162 Sagittary (An inn where Othello and Desdemona are staying.)
raisèd search search party roused out of sleep   **163 s.d. nightgown**
dressing gown. (This costuming is specified in the quarto text.)   **165 time**
i.e., remainder of life   **175 charms** spells   **176 property** special quality,
nature   **177 abused** deceived   **182 discover** reveal, uncover

BRABANTIO
Pray you, lead on. At every house I'll call;
I may command at most.—Get weapons, ho!   185
And raise some special officers of night.—
On, good Roderigo. I will deserve your pains.   187

Exeunt.

✤

1.2   *Enter Othello, Iago, attendants with torches.*

IAGO
Though in the trade of war I have slain men,
Yet do I hold it very stuff o' the conscience   2
To do no contrived murder. I lack iniquity   3
Sometimes to do me service. Nine or ten times
I had thought t' have yerked him here under the ribs.   5
OTHELLO
'Tis better as it is.
IAGO   Nay, but he prated,
And spoke such scurvy and provoking terms
Against your honor
That, with the little godliness I have,
I did full hard forbear him. But, I pray you, sir,   10
Are you fast married? Be assured of this,
That the magnifico is much beloved,   12
And hath in his effect a voice potential   13
As double as the Duke's. He will divorce you,   14
Or put upon you what restraint and grievance
The law, with all his might to enforce it on,
Will give him cable.
OTHELLO   Let him do his spite.   17
My services which I have done the seigniory   18

---

185 command demand assistance   **187 deserve** show gratitude for

1.2. Location: Venice. Another street, before Othello's lodgings.
2 very stuff essence, basic material (continuing the metaphor of *trade*
from l. 1)   **3 contrived** premeditated   **5 yerked** stabbed.   **him** i.e.,
Roderigo   **10 I . . . him** I restrained myself with great difficulty from
assaulting him   **12 magnifico** Venetian grandee, i.e., Brabantio   **13 in
his effect** at his command.   **potential** powerful   **14 double** doubly
powerful (in comparison with other senators)   **17 cable** i.e., scope
18 seigniory Venetian government

Shall out-tongue his complaints. 'Tis yet to know—   19
Which, when I know that boasting is an honor,
I shall promulgate—I fetch my life and being
From men of royal siege, and my demerits   22
May speak unbonneted to as proud a fortune   23
As this that I have reached. For know, Iago,
But that I love the gentle Desdemona,
I would not my unhousèd free condition   26
Put into circumscription and confine   27
For the sea's worth. But look, what lights come yond? 28

Enter Cassio [and certain Officers] with torches.

IAGO
Those are the raisèd father and his friends.
You were best go in.
OTHELLO   Not I. I must be found.
My parts, my title, and my perfect soul   31
Shall manifest me rightly. Is it they?
IAGO   By Janus, I think no.   33
OTHELLO
The servants of the Duke? And my lieutenant?
The goodness of the night upon you, friends!
What is the news?
CASSIO   The Duke does greet you, General,
And he requires your haste-post-haste appearance
Even on the instant.
OTHELLO   What is the matter, think you?   38
CASSIO
Something from Cyprus, as I may divine.•   39
It is a business of some heat. The galleys   40
Have sent a dozen sequent messengers   41
This very night at one another's heels,

---

19 yet to know not yet widely known   **22 siege** i.e., rank. (Literally, a
seat used by a person of distinction.)   **demerits** deserts   **23 unbonneted**
without removing the hat, i.e., on equal terms (? Or "with hat off," "in
all due modesty.")   **26 unhousèd** unconfined, undomesticated   **27 circumscription and confine** restriction and confinement   **28 the sea's
worth** all the riches at the bottom of the sea   **s.d. Officers** (The quarto
text calls for "Cassio with lights, officers with torches.")   **31 My . . .
soul** my natural gifts, my position or reputation, and my unflawed
conscience   **33 Janus** Roman two-faced god of beginnings   **38 matter**
business   **39 divine** guess   **40 heat** urgency   **41 sequent** successive

And many of the consuls, raised and met,   43
Are at the Duke's already. You have been hotly called for;
When, being not at your lodging to be found,
The Senate hath sent about three several quests   46
To search you out.
OTHELLO   'Tis well I am found by you.
I will but spend a word here in the house
And go with you.   [*Exit.*]
CASSIO   Ancient, what makes he here?   49
IAGO
Faith, he tonight hath boarded a land carrack.   50
If it prove lawful prize, he's made forever.   51
CASSIO
I do not understand.
IAGO   He's married.
CASSIO   To who?

        [*Enter Othello.*]

IAGO
Marry, to—Come, Captain, will you go?   53
OTHELLO   Have with you.   54
CASSIO
Here comes another troop to seek for you.   55

        *Enter Brabantio, Roderigo, with officers and
        torches.*

IAGO
It is Brabantio. General, be advised.   56
He comes to bad intent.
OTHELLO   Holla! Stand there!
RODERIGO
Signor, it is the Moor.
BRABANTIO   Down with him, thief!
                    [*They draw on both sides.*]
IAGO
You, Roderigo! Come, sir, I am for you.

43 consuls senators   **46 several** separate   **49 makes** does   **50 boarded**
gone aboard and seized as an act of piracy (with sexual suggestion).
carrack large merchant ship   **51 prize** booty   **53 Marry** (An oath,
originally "by the Virgin Mary.")   **54 Have with you** i.e., let's go
55 s.d. officers and torches (The quarto text calls for "others with lights
and weapons.")   **56 be advised** be on your guard

OTHELLO
  Keep up your bright swords, for the dew will rust them. 60
  Good signor, you shall more command with years
  Than with your weapons.
BRABANTIO
  O thou foul thief, where hast thou stowed my daughter?
  Damned as thou art, thou hast enchanted her!
  For I'll refer me to all things of sense,   65
  If she in chains of magic were not bound
  Whether a maid so tender, fair, and happy,
  So opposite to marriage that she shunned
  The wealthy curlèd darlings of our nation,
  Would ever have, t' incur a general mock,
  Run from her guardage to the sooty bosom   71
  Of such a thing as thou—to fear, not to delight.
  Judge me the world if 'tis not gross in sense   73
  That thou hast practiced on her with foul charms,
  Abused her delicate youth with drugs or minerals   75
  That weakens motion. I'll have 't disputed on;   76
  'Tis probable, and palpable to thinking.
  I therefore apprehend and do attach thee   78
  For an abuser of the world, a practicer
  Of arts inhibited and out of warrant.—   80
  Lay hold upon him! If he do resist,
  Subdue him at his peril.
OTHELLO   Hold your hands,
  Both you of my inclining and the rest.   83
  Were it my cue to fight, I should have known it
  Without a prompter.—Whither will you that I go
  To answer this your charge?
BRABANTIO   To prison, till fit time
  Of law and course of direct session   88
  Call thee to answer.
OTHELLO   What if I do obey?

---

60 Keep up i.e., sheathe   **65 refer me** submit my case.   **things of sense**
commonsense understandings, or, creatures possessing common
sense   **71 guardage** guardianship   **73 gross in sense** obvious   **75 min**
erals i.e., poisons   **76 weakens motion** impair the vital faculties.
disputed on argued in court by professional counsel, discussed by
experts   **78 attach** arrest   **80 inhibited** prohibited.   **out of warrant**
illegal   **83 inclining** following, party   **88 course of direct session**
regular or specially convened legal proceedings

How may the Duke be therewith satisfied,
Whose messengers are here about my side
Upon some present business of the state
To bring me to him?
OFFICER   'Tis true, most worthy signor.
The Duke's in council, and your noble self,
I am sure, is sent for.
BRABANTIO   How? The Duke in council?
In this time of the night? Bring him away.   96
Mine's not an idle cause. The Duke himself,   97
Or any of my brothers of the state,
Cannot but feel this wrong as 'twere their own;
For if such actions may have passage free,
Bondslaves and pagans shall our statesmen be.

                                       Exeunt.

❖

1.3   *Enter Duke [and] Senators [and sit at a table,*
          with lights], and Officers. [The Duke and
          Senators are reading dispatches.]

DUKE
There is no composition in these news   1
That gives them credit.
FIRST SENATOR   Indeed, they are disproportioned.   3
My letters say a hundred and seven galleys.
DUKE
And mine, a hundred forty.
SECOND SENATOR   And mine, two hundred.
But though they jump not on a just account—   6
As in these cases, where the aim reports   7
'Tis oft with difference—yet do they all confirm
A Turkish fleet, and bearing up to Cyprus.
DUKE
Nay, it is possible enough to judgment.

---

96 **away** right along   97 **idle** trifling

1.3. Location: Venice. A council chamber.
s.d. Enter . . . Officers (The quarto text calls for the Duke and Senators
to "sit at a table with lights and attendants.")   1 **composition** consis-
tency   3 **disproportioned** inconsistent   6 **jump** agree. **just** exact
7 **the aim** conjecture

I do not so secure me in the error 11
But the main article I do approve 12
In fearful sense.

SAILOR (*Within*)　　What ho, what ho, what ho!

　　　Enter Sailor.

OFFICER　A messenger from the galleys.
DUKE　Now, what's the business?
SAILOR
The Turkish preparation makes for Rhodes. 16
So was I bid report here to the state
By Signor Angelo.
DUKE
How say you by this change?
FIRST SENATOR　　　　　　　This cannot be 19
By no assay of reason. 'Tis a pageant 20
To keep us in false gaze. When we consider 21
Th' importancy of Cyprus to the Turk,
And let ourselves again but understand
That, as it more concerns the Turk than Rhodes,
So may he with more facile question bear it, 25
For that it stands not in such warlike brace, 26
But altogether lacks th' abilities 27
That Rhodes is dressed in—if we make thought of this, 28
We must not think the Turk is so unskillful 29
To leave that latest which concerns him first, 30
Neglecting an attempt of ease and gain
To wake and wage a danger profitless. 32
DUKE
Nay, in all confidence, he's not for Rhodes.
OFFICER　Here is more news.

　　　Enter a Messenger.

11–12 **I do not . . . approve** I do not take such (false) comfort in the
discrepancies that I fail to perceive the main point, i.e., that the Turkish
fleet is threatening　**16 preparation** fleet prepared for battle　**19 by**
about　**20 assay** test.　**pageant** mere show　**21 in false gaze** looking the
wrong way　**25 may . . . it** he (the Turk) can more easily capture it
(Cyprus)　**26 For that** since.　**brace** state of defense　**27 abilities** means
of self-defense　**28 dressed in** equipped with　**29 unskillful** deficient in
judgment　**30 latest** last　**32 wake** stir up.　**wage** risk

MESSENGER

    The Ottomites, reverend and gracious,
    Steering with due course toward the isle of Rhodes,
    Have there injointed them with an after fleet.   37

FIRST SENATOR

    Ay, so I thought. How many, as you guess?

MESSENGER

    Of thirty sail; and now they do restem   39
    Their backward course, bearing with frank appearance   40
    Their purposes toward Cyprus. Signor Montano,
    Your trusty and most valiant servitor,   42
    With his free duty recommends you thus,   43
    And prays you to believe him.

DUKE   'Tis certain then for Cyprus.

    Marcus Luccicos, is not he in town?

FIRST SENATOR   He's now in Florence.

DUKE

    Write from us to him, post-post-haste. Dispatch.

FIRST SENATOR

    Here comes Brabantio and the valiant Moor.

        Enter Brabantio, Othello, Cassio, Iago, Roderigo,
        and officers.

DUKE

    Valiant Othello, we must straight employ you   50
    Against the general enemy Ottoman.   51
    [*To Brabantio.*] I did not see you; welcome, gentle signor. 52
    We lacked your counsel and your help tonight.

BRABANTIO

    So did I yours. Good Your Grace, pardon me;
    Neither my place nor aught I heard of business   55
    Hath raised me from my bed, nor doth the general care
    Take hold on me, for my particular grief   57
    Is of so floodgate and o'erbearing nature   58

---

37 injointed them joined themselves.   **after** second   **39–40 restem . . .
course** retrace their original course   **40 frank appearance** i.e., undis-
guised intent   **42 servitor** officer under your command   **43 free duty**
freely given and loyal service.   **recommends** commends himself and
reports to   **50 straight** straightway   **51 general** universal, i.e., against
all Christendom   **52 gentle** noble   **55 place** official position
57 particular personal   **58 floodgate** i.e., overwhelming (as when flood-
gates are opened)

That it engluts and swallows other sorrows   59
And it is still itself.
DUKE   Why, what's the matter?   60
BRABANTIO
My daughter! O, my daughter!
DUKE AND SENATORS   Dead?
BRABANTIO   Ay, to me.
She is abused, stol'n from me, and corrupted   62
By spells and medicines bought of mountebanks;
For nature so preposterously to err,
Being not deficient, blind, or lame of sense,   65
Sans witchcraft could not.   66
DUKE
Whoe'er he be that in this foul proceeding
Hath thus beguiled your daughter of herself,
And you of her, the bloody book of law
You shall yourself read in the bitter letter
After your own sense—yea, though our proper son   71
Stood in your action.
BRABANTIO   Humbly I thank Your Grace.   72
Here is the man, this Moor, whom now it seems
Your special mandate for the state affairs
Hath hither brought.
ALL   We are very sorry for 't.
DUKE [*To Othello*]
What, in your own part, can you say to this?
BRABANTIO   Nothing, but this is so.
OTHELLO
Most potent, grave, and reverend signors,
My very noble and approved good masters: 79
That I have ta'en away this old man's daughter,
It is most true; true, I have married her.
The very head and front of my offending   82
Hath this extent, no more. Rude am I in my speech,   83
And little blessed with the soft phrase of peace;
For since these arms of mine had seven years' pith,   85

59 engluts engulfs   60 is still itself remains undiminished   62 abused
deceived   65 deficient defective   66 Sans without   71 After . . . sense
according to your own interpretation.   our proper my own   72 Stood
. . action were under your accusation   79 approved proved, es-
teemed   82 head and front height and breadth, entire extent   83 Rude
unpolished   85 pith strength, vigor (i.e., since I was seven)

Till now some nine moons wasted, they have used   86
Their dearest action in the tented field;   87
And little of this great world can I speak
More than pertains to feats of broils and battle,
And therefore little shall I grace my cause.
In speaking for myself. Yet, by your gracious patience,
I will a round unvarnished tale deliver   92
Of my whole course of love—what drugs, what charms,
What conjuration, and what mighty magic,
For such proceeding I am charged withal,   95
I won his daughter.
BRABANTIO   A maiden never bold;
Of spirit so still and quiet that her motion   97
Blushed at herself; and she, in spite of nature,   98
Of years, of country, credit, everything,   99
To fall in love with what she feared to look on!
It is a judgment maimed and most imperfect
That will confess perfection so could err   102
Against all rules of nature, and must be driven
To find out practices of cunning hell   104
Why this should be. I therefore vouch again   105
That with some mixtures powerful o'er the blood,   106
Or with some dram conjured to this effect,   107
He wrought upon her.
DUKE   To vouch this is no proof,
Without more wider and more overt test   109
Than these thin habits and poor likelihoods   110
Of modern seeming do prefer against him.   111
FIRST SENATOR   But, Othello, speak.
Did you by indirect and forcèd courses
Subdue and poison this young maid's affections?
Or came it by request and such fair question   115
As soul to soul affordeth?

86 Till . . . wasted until some nine months ago (since when Othello
has evidently not been on active duty, but in Venice)   **87 dearest** most
valuable   **92 round** plain   **95 withal** with   **97–98 her . . . herself** her
very emotions prompted her to blush at discovering such feelings in
herself   **99 years** i.e., difference in age.   **credit** virtuous reputation
102 confess concede (that)   **104 practices** plots   **105 vouch** assert
106 blood passions   **107 conjured to this effect** made by magical spells
to have this effect   **109 more wider** fuller   **110 habits** garments, i.e.,
appearances   **111 modern seeming** commonplace assumption.   **prefer**
bring forth   **115 question** conversation

OTHELLO   I do beseech you,
Send for the lady to the Sagittary
And let her speak of me before her father.
If you do find me foul in her report,
The trust, the office I do hold of you
Not only take away, but let your sentence
Even fall upon my life.
DUKE   Fetch Desdemona hither.
OTHELLO
Ancient, conduct them. You best know the place.
                    [*Exeunt Iago and attendants.*]
And, till she come, as truly as to heaven
I do confess the vices of my blood,   125
So justly to your grave ears I'll present   126
How I did thrive in this fair lady's love,
And she in mine.
DUKE   Say it, Othello.
OTHELLO
Her father loved me, oft invited me,
Still questioned me the story of my life   131
From year to year—the battles, sieges, fortunes,
That I have passed.
I ran it through, even from my boyish days
To th' very moment that he bade me tell it,
Wherein I spoke of most disastrous chances,
Of moving accidents by flood and field,   137
Of hairbreadth scapes i' th' imminent deadly breach,   138
Of being taken by the insolent foe
And sold to slavery, of my redemption thence,
And portance in my travels' history,   141
Wherein of antres vast and deserts idle,   142
Rough quarries, rocks, and hills whose heads touch
    heaven,   143
It was my hint to speak—such was my process—   144
And of the Cannibals that each other eat,
The Anthropophagi, and men whose heads   146

125 blood passions, human nature **126 justly** truthfully, accurately
131 Still continually **137 accidents** happenings **138 imminent . . .
breach** death-threatening gaps made in a fortification **141 portance**
conduct **142 antres** caverns. **idle** barren, desolate **143 Rough
quarries** rugged rock formations **144 hint** occasion, opportunity
146 Anthropophagi man-eaters. (A term from Pliny's *Natural History*.)

Do grow beneath their shoulders. These things to hear
Would Desdemona seriously incline;
But still the house affairs would draw her thence,
Which ever as she could with haste dispatch
She'd come again, and with a greedy ear
Devour up my discourse. Which I, observing,
Took once a pliant hour, and found good means   153
To draw from her a prayer of earnest heart
That I would all my pilgrimage dilate,   155
Whereof by parcels she had something heard,   156
But not intentively. I did consent,   157
And often did beguile her of her tears,
When I did speak of some distressful stroke
That my youth suffered. My story being done,
She gave me for my pains a world of sighs.
She swore, in faith, 'twas strange, 'twas passing strange, 162
'Twas pitiful, 'twas wondrous pitiful.
She wished she had not heard it, yet she wished
That heaven had made her such a man. She thanked me,
And bade me, if I had a friend that loved her,
I should but teach him how to tell my story,
And that would woo her. Upon this hint I spake.   168
She loved me for the dangers I had passed,
And I loved her that she did pity them.
This only is the witchcraft I have used.
Here comes the lady. Let her witness it.

        Enter Desdemona, Iago, [and] attendants.

DUKE
I think this tale would win my daughter too.
Good Brabantio,
Take up this mangled matter at the best.   175
Men do their broken weapons rather use
Than their bare hands.
BRABANTIO   I pray you, hear her speak.
If she confess that she was half the wooer,
Destruction on my head if my bad blame

---

153 pliant well-suiting **155 dilate** relate in detail **156 by parcels**
piecemeal **157 intentively** with full attention **162 passing** exceedingly **168 hint** opportunity **175 Take . . . best** make the best of a bad
bargain

Light on the man!—Come hither, gentle mistress.
Do you perceive in all this noble company
Where most you owe obedience?

DESDEMONA   My noble Father,
I do perceive here a divided duty.
To you I am bound for life and education;   184
My life and education both do learn me   185
How to respect you. You are the lord of duty;
I am hitherto your daughter. But here's my husband,
And so much duty as my mother showed
To you, preferring you before her father,
So much I challenge that I may profess   190
Due to the Moor my lord.

BRABANTIO   God be with you! I have done.
Please it Your Grace, on to the state affairs.
I had rather to adopt a child than get it.   194
Come hither, Moor.   [*He joins the hands of Othello
                            and Desdemona.*]
I here do give thee that with all my heart   196
Which, but thou hast already, with all my heart   197
I would keep from thee.—For your sake, jewel,   198
I am glad at soul I have no other child,
For thy escape would teach me tyranny,   200
To hang clogs on them.—I have done, my lord.   201

DUKE
Let me speak like yourself, and lay a sentence   202
Which, as a grece or step, may help these lovers   203
Into your favor.
When remedies are past, the griefs are ended   205
By seeing the worst, which late on hopes depended.   206
To mourn a mischief that is past and gone   207
Is the next way to draw new mischief on.   208

---

184 education upbringing   **185 learn** teach   **190 challenge** claim
194 get beget   **196 with all my heart** wherein my whole affection has
been engaged   **197 with all my heart** willingly, gladly   **198 For your
sake** on your account   **200 escape** elopement   **201 clogs** (Literally,
blocks of wood fastened to the legs of criminals or convicts to inhibit
escape.)   **202 like yourself** i.e., as you would, in your proper temper.
sentence maxim (also at l. 219)   **203 grece** step   **205 remedies** hopes of
remedy   **206 which** i.e., the griefs.   **late . . . depended** were sustained
until recently by hopeful anticipation   **207 mischief** misfortune, injury   **208 next** nearest

What cannot be preserved when fortune takes,   209
Patience her injury a mockery makes.   210
The robbed that smiles steals something from the thief;
He robs himself that spends a bootless grief.   212

BRABANTIO
So let the Turk of Cyprus us beguile,
We lose it not, so long as we can smile.
He bears the sentence well that nothing bears   215
But the free comfort which from thence he hears,   216
But he bears both the sentence and the sorrow   217
That, to pay grief, must of poor patience borrow.   218
These sentences, to sugar or to gall,   219
Being strong on both sides, are equivocal.   220
But words are words. I never yet did hear
That the bruised heart was piercèd through the ear.   222
I humbly beseech you, proceed to th' affairs of state.

DUKE   The Turk with a most mighty preparation makes
for Cyprus. Othello, the fortitude of the place is best   225
known to you; and though we have there a substitute   226
of most allowed sufficiency, yet opinion, a sovereign   227
mistress of effects, throws a more safer voice on you.   228
You must therefore be content to slubber the gloss of   229
your new fortunes with this more stubborn and   230
boisterous expedition.

OTHELLO
The tyrant custom, most grave senators,
Hath made the flinty and steel couch of war
My thrice-driven bed of down. I do agnize   234

---

209 What whatever   **210 Patience . . . makes** patience laughs at the
injury inflicted by fortune (and thus eases the pain)   **212 spends a
bootless grief** indulges in unavailing grief   **215–218 He bears . . .
borrow** i.e., a person well bears out your maxim who takes with him
only the philosophic consolation it teaches him, a comfort free from
sorrow; but anyone whose grief bankrupts his poor patience is left with
your saying and his sorrow too. (*Bears the sentence* also plays on the
meaning, "receives judicial sentence.")   **219–220 These . . . equivocal**
i.e., these fine maxims are equivocal, either sweet or bitter in their
application   **222 piercèd . . . ear** i.e., surgically lanced and cured by
mere words of advice   **225 fortitude** strength   **226 substitute** deputy
227 allowed acknowledged   **227–228 opinion . . . on you** general opinion, an important determiner of affairs, chooses you as the best man
229 slubber soil, sully   **230 stubborn** harsh, rough   **234 thrice-driven**
thrice sifted, winnowed.   **agnize** know in myself, acknowledge

A natural and prompt alacrity
I find in hardness, and do undertake   236
These present wars against the Ottomites.
Most humbly therefore bending to your state,   238
I crave fit disposition for my wife,
Due reference of place and exhibition,   240
With such accommodation and besort   241
As levels with her breeding.   242

DUKE
  Why, at her father's.

BRABANTIO   I will not have it so.

OTHELLO
  Nor I.

DESDEMONA   Nor I. I would not there reside,
  To put my father in impatient thoughts
  By being in his eye. Most gracious Duke,
  To my unfolding lend your prosperous ear,   247
  And let me find a charter in your voice   248
  T' assist my simpleness.

DUKE   What would you, Desdemona?

DESDEMONA
  That I did love the Moor to live with him,
  My downright violence and storm of fortunes   252
  May trumpet to the world. My heart's subdued   253
  Even to the very quality of my lord.   254
  I saw Othello's visage in his mind,
  And to his honors and his valiant parts   256
  Did I my soul and fortunes consecrate.
  So that, dear lords, if I be left behind
  A moth of peace, and he go to the war,   259
  The rites for why I love him are bereft me,   260
  And I a heavy interim shall support

236 hardness hardship   **238 bending . . . state** bowing or kneeling to
your authority   **240 reference . . . exhibition** provision of place to live
and allowance of money   **241 accommodation** suitable provision.
besort attendance   **242 levels** equals, suits   **247 unfolding** explanation,
proposal.   **prosperous** propitious   **248 charter** privilege, authorization   **252 My . . . fortunes** my plain and total breach of social custom,
taking my future by storm and disrupting my whole life   **253–254 My
heart's . . . lord** my heart is brought wholly into accord with Othello's
virtues; I love him for his virtues   **256 parts** qualities   **259 moth** i.e.,
one who consumes merely   **260 rites** rites of love (with a suggestion too
of *rights*, sharing)

By his dear absence. Let me go with him.   262
OTHELLO   Let her have your voice.   263
Vouch with me, heaven, I therefor beg it not
To please the palate of my appetite,
Nor to comply with heat—the young affects   266
In me defunct—and proper satisfaction,   267
But to be free and bounteous to her mind.   268
And heaven defend your good souls that you think   269
I will your serious and great business scant
When she is with me. No, when light-winged toys
Of feathered Cupid seel with wanton dullness   272
My speculative and officed instruments,   273
That my disports corrupt and taint my business,   274
Let huswives make a skillet of my helm,
And all indign and base adversities   276
Make head against my estimation!   277
DUKE
Be it as you shall privately determine,
Either for her stay or going. Th' affair cries haste,
And speed must answer it.
A SENATOR   You must away tonight.
DESDEMONA
Tonight, my lord?
DUKE   This night.
OTHELLO   With all my heart.
DUKE
At nine i' the morning here we'll meet again.
Othello, leave some officer behind,
And he shall our commission bring to you,
With such things else of quality and respect   285
As doth import you.
OTHELLO   So please Your Grace, my ancient; 286
A man he is of honesty and trust.

---

262 dear (1) heartfelt (2) costly   **263 voice** consent   **266 heat** sexual
passion.   **young affects** passions of youth, desires   **267 proper** personal   **268 free** generous   **269 defend** forbid.   **think** should think
272 seel i.e., make blind (as in falconry, by sewing up the eyes of the
hawk during training)   **273 speculative . . . instruments** i.e., perceptive
faculties used in the performance of duty   **274 That** so that.   **disports**
sexual pastimes.   **taint** impair   **276 indign** unworthy, shameful
277 Make head raise an army.   **estimation** reputation   **285 of quality
and respect** of importance and relevance   **286 import** concern

To his conveyance I assign my wife,
With what else need^ful Your Good Grace shall think
To be sent after me.

DUKE   Let it be so.
  Good night to everyone. [*To Brabantio.*] And, noble
    signor,
  If virtue no delighted beauty lack,   292
  Your son-in-law is far more fair than black.

FIRST SENATOR
  Adieu, brave Moor. Use Desdemona well.

BRABANTIO
  Look to her, Moor, if thou hast eyes to see.
  She has deceived her father, and may thee.
          Exeunt [*Duke, Brabantio, Cassio, Senators,*
                            and Officers].

OTHELLO
  My life upon her faith! Honest Iago,
  My Desdemona must I leave to thee.
  I prithee, let thy wife attend on her,
  And bring them after in the best advantage.   300
  Come, Desdemona. I have but an hour
  Of love, of worldly matters and direction,   302
  To spend with thee. We must obey the time.
                    Exit [*with Desdemona*].

RODERIGO Iago—

IAGO What sayst thou, noble heart?

RODERIGO What will I do, think'st thou?

IAGO Why, go to bed and sleep.

RODERIGO I will incontinently drown myself.   308

IAGO If thou dost, I shall never love thee after. Why,
  thou silly gentleman?

RODERIGO It is silliness to live when to live is torment;
  and then have we a prescription to die when death is   312
  our physician.

IAGO O villainous! I have looked upon the world for 314
  four times seven years, and, since I could distinguish
  betwixt a benefit and an injury, I never found man

292 delighted capable of delighting   **300 in . . . advantage** at the most
favorable opportunity   **302 direction** instructions   **308 incontinently**
immediately   **312 prescription** (1) right based on long-established
custom (2) doctor's prescription   **314 villainous** i.e., what perfect
nonsense

that knew how to love himself. Ere I would say I
would drown myself for the love of a guinea hen, I   318
would change my humanity with a baboon.

RODERIGO   What should I do? I confess it is my shame
to be so fond, but it is not in my virtue to amend it.   321

IAGO   Virtue? A fig! 'Tis in ourselves that we are thus or   322
thus. Our bodies are our gardens, to the which our
wills are gardeners; so that if we will plant nettles or
sow lettuce, set hyssop and weed up thyme, supply it   325
with one gender of herbs or distract it with many, ei-   326
ther to have it sterile with idleness or manured with   327
industry—why, the power and corrigible authority of   328
this lies in our wills. If the beam of our lives had not   329
one scale of reason to poise another of sensuality, the   330
blood and baseness of our natures would conduct us   331
to most preposterous conclusions. But we have reason
to cool our raging motions, our carnal stings, our un-   333
bitted lusts, whereof I take this that you call love to be   334
a sect or scion.   335

RODERIGO   It cannot be.

IAGO   It is merely a lust of the blood and a permission
of the will. Come, be a man. Drown thyself? Drown
cats and blind puppies. I have professed me thy friend,
and I confess me knit to thy deserving with cables of
perdurable toughness. I could never better stead thee   341
than now. Put money in thy purse. Follow thou the
wars; defeat thy favor with an usurped beard. I say,   343
put money in thy purse. It cannot be long that Desdemona should continue her love to the Moor—put
money in thy purse—nor he his to her. It was a vio-

---

318 **guinea hen** (A slang term for a prostitute.)   321 **fond** infatuated.
virtue strength, nature   322 **fig** (To give a fig is to thrust the thumb
between the first and second fingers in a vulgar and insulting gesture.)   325 **hyssop** a herb of the mint family   326 **gender** kind.
distract it with divide it among   327 **idleness** want of cultivation
328 **corrigible authority** power to correct   329 **beam** balance
330 **poise** counterbalance   331 **blood** natural passions   333 **motions**
appetites   333–334 **unbitted** unbridled, uncontrolled   335 **sect or scion**
cutting or offshoot   341 **perdurable** very durable.   **stead** assist
343 **defeat thy favor** disguise your face.   **usurped** (The suggestion is
that Roderigo is not man enough to have a beard of his own.)

lent commencement in her, and thou shalt see an an- 347
swerable sequestration—put but money in thy purse. 348
These Moors are changeable in their wills—fill thy 349
purse with money. The food that to him now is as ⎫
luscious as locusts shall be to him shortly as bitter as ⎬351
coloquintida. She must change for youth; when she is ⎭352
sated with his body, she will find the error of her
choice. She must have change, she must. Therefore
put money in thy purse. If thou wilt needs damn thyself, do it a more delicate way than drowning. Make 356
all the money thou canst. If sanctimony and a frail vow 357
betwixt an erring barbarian and a supersubtle Vene- 358
tian be not too hard for my wits and all the tribe of
hell, thou shalt enjoy her. Therefore make money. A
pox of drowning thyself! It is clean out of the way.
Seek thou rather to be hanged in compassing thy joy 362
than to be drowned and go without her.

RODERIGO Wilt thou be fast to my hopes if I depend on 364
the issue?

IAGO Thou art sure of me. Go, make money. I have
told thee often, and I retell thee again and again, I hate
the Moor. My cause is hearted; thine hath no less rea- 368
son. Let us be conjunctive in our revenge against him. 369
If thou canst cuckold him, thou dost thyself a pleasure,
me a sport. There are many events in the womb of
time which will be delivered. Traverse, go, provide thy 372
money. We will have more of this tomorrow. Adieu.

RODERIGO Where shall we meet i' the morning?

IAGO At my lodging.

RODERIGO I'll be with thee betimes. [*He starts to leave.*] 376

IAGO Go to, farewell.—Do you hear, Roderigo?

RODERIGO What say you?

IAGO No more of drowning, do you hear?

347–348 an answerable sequestration a corresponding separation or
estrangement   **349 wills** carnal appetites   **351 locusts** fruit of the carob
tree (see Matthew 3:4), or perhaps honeysuckle   **352 coloquintida**
colocynth or bitter apple, a purgative   **356 Make** raise, collect
357 sanctimony sacred ceremony   **358 erring** wandering, vagabond,
unsteady   **362 compassing** encompassing, embracing   **364 fast** true
368 hearted fixed in the heart, heartfelt   **369 conjunctive** united
372 Traverse (A military marching term.)   **376 betimes** early

RODERIGO   I am changed.

IAGO   Go to, farewell. Put money enough in your
purse.

RODERIGO   I'll sell all my land.   *Exit.*

IAGO

Thus do I ever make my fool my purse;
For I mine own gained knowledge should profane
If I would time expend with such a snipe   386
But for my sport and profit. I hate the Moor;
And it is thought abroad that twixt my sheets   388
He's done my office. I know not if 't be true;   389
But I, for mere suspicion in that kind,
Will do as if for surety. He holds me well;   391
The better shall my purpose work on him.
Cassio's a proper man. Let me see now: 393
To get his place and to plume up my will   394
In double knavery—How, how?—Let's see:
After some time, to abuse Othello's ear   396
That he is too familiar with his wife.   397
He hath a person and a smooth dispose   398
To be suspected, framed to make women false.
The Moor is of a free and open nature,   400
That thinks men honest that but seem to be so,
And will as tenderly be led by the nose   402
As asses are.
I have 't. It is engendered. Hell and night
Must bring this monstrous birth to the world's light.
                                                              [*Exit.*]

❖

386 **snipe** woodcock, i.e., fool   388 **it is thought abroad** i.e., it is rumored   389 **my office** i.e., my sexual function as husband   391 **do . . .
surety** act as if on certain knowledge.   **holds me well** regards me
favorably   393 **proper** handsome   394 **plume up** glorify, gratify
396 **abuse** deceive   397 **he** i.e., Cassio   398 **dispose** manner, bearing
400 **free** frank, generous.   **open** unsuspicious   402 **tenderly** readily

Enter Montano and two Gentlemen.

MONTANO
  What from the cape can you discern at sea?
FIRST GENTLEMAN
  Nothing at all. It is a high-wrought flood.   2
  I cannot, twixt the heaven and the main,   3
  Descry a sail.
MONTANO
  Methinks the wind hath spoke aloud at land;
  A fuller blast ne'er shook our battlements.
  If it hath ruffianed so upon the sea,   7
  What ribs of oak, when mountains melt on them,   8
  Can hold the mortise? What shall we hear of this?   9
SECOND GENTLEMAN
  A segregation of the Turkish fleet.   10
  For do but stand upon the foaming shore,
  The chidden billow seems to pelt the clouds;   12
  The wind-shaked surge, with high and monstrous mane,   13
  Seems to cast water on the burning Bear   14
  And quench the guards of th' ever-fixèd pole.
  I never did like molestation view   16
  On the enchafèd flood.   17
MONTANO   If that the Turkish fleet   18
  Be not ensheltered and embayed, they are drowned;   19
  It is impossible to bear it out.   20

      Enter a [Third] Gentleman.

THIRD GENTLEMAN   News, lads! Our wars are done.

2.1. Location: A seaport in Cyprus. An open place near the quay.
high-wrought flood very agitated sea   **3 main** ocean (also at l. 41)
ruffianed raged   **8 mountains** i.e., of water   **9 hold the mortise** hold
their joints together. (A *mortise* is the socket hollowed out in fitting
timbers.)   **10 segregation** dispersion   **12 chidden** i.e., rebuked, repelled
(by the shore), and thus shot into the air   **13 monstrous mane** (The surf
is like the mane of a wild beast.)   **14 the burning Bear** i.e., the constel-
lation Ursa Minor or the Little Bear, which includes the polestar (and
hence regarded as the *guards of th' ever-fixèd pole* in the next line;
sometimes the term *guards* is applied to the two "pointers" of the Big
Bear or Dipper, which may be intended here.)   **16 like molestation**
comparable uproar   **17 enchafèd** angry   **18 If that** if   **19 embayed**
sheltered by a bay   **20 bear it out** survive, weather the storm

The desperate tempest hath so banged the Turks
That their designment halts. A noble ship of Venice   23
Hath seen a grievous wreck and sufferance   24
On most part of their fleet.
MONTANO   How? Is this true?
THIRD GENTLEMAN   The ship is here put in,
A Veronesa; Michael Cassio,   28
Lieutenant to the warlike Moor Othello,
Is come on shore; the Moor himself at sea,
And is in full commission here for Cyprus.
MONTANO
I am glad on 't. 'Tis a worthy governor.
THIRD GENTLEMAN
But this same Cassio, though he speak of comfort
Touching the Turkish loss, yet he looks sadly   34
And prays the Moor be safe, for they were parted
With foul and violent tempest.
MONTANO   Pray heaven he be,
For I have served him, and the man commands
Like a full soldier. Let's to the seaside, ho!   38
As well to see the vessel that's come in
As to throw out our eyes for brave Othello,
Even till we make the main and th' aerial blue   41
An indistinct regard.
THIRD GENTLEMAN   Come, let's do so,   42
For every minute is expectancy   43
Of more arrivance.   44

      Enter Cassio.

CASSIO
Thanks, you the valiant of this warlike isle,
That so approve the Moor! O, let the heavens   46
Give him defense against the elements,
For I have lost him on a dangerous sea.
MONTANO   Is he well shipped?

23 **designment** enterprise. **halts** is lame   24 **wreck** shipwreck.
sufferance disaster   28 **Veronesa** i.e., fitted out in Verona for Venetian
service, or possibly *Verennessa* (the Folio spelling), a cutter (from *ver-
rinare*, to cut through)   34 **sadly** gravely   38 **full** perfect   41 **the main
. . . blue** the sea and the sky   42 **An indistinct regard** indistinguishable
in our view   43 **is expectancy** gives expectation   44 **arrivance** arrival
46 approve admire, honor

CASSIO
His bark is stoutly timbered, and his pilot
Of very expert and approved allowance;   51
Therefore my hopes, not surfeited to death,   52
Stand in bold cure.
                [*A cry*] *within:* "A sail, a sail, a sail!" 53
CASSIO   What noise?
A GENTLEMAN
The town is empty. On the brow o' the sea
Stand ranks of people, and they cry "A sail!"
CASSIO
My hopes do shape him for the governor.
                        [*A shot within.*]
SECOND GENTLEMAN
They do discharge their shot of courtesy;   58
Our friends at least.
CASSIO   I pray you, sir, go forth,
And give us truth who 'tis that is arrived.
SECOND GENTLEMAN   I shall.   *Exit.*
MONTANO
But, good Lieutenant, is your general wived?
CASSIO
Most fortunately. He hath achieved a maid
That paragons description and wild fame,   64
One that excels the quirks of blazoning pens,   65
And in th' essential vesture of creation   66
Does tire the enginer.

    Enter [*Second*] *Gentleman.*

                    How now? Who has put in?   67
SECOND GENTLEMAN
'Tis one Iago, ancient to the General.

---

51 approved allowance tested reputation **52 surfeited to death** i.e.,
overextended, worn thin through repeated application or delayed fulfillment **53 in bold cure** in strong hopes of fulfillment **58 discharge ...
courtesy** fire a salute in token of respect and courtesy **64 paragons**
surpasses. **wild fame** extravagant report **65 quirks** witty conceits.
blazoning setting forth as though in heraldic language **66–67 in ...
enginer** in her real beauty (she) defeats any attempt to praise her.
enginer engineer, i.e., poet, one who devises **s.d. Second Gentleman**
(So identified in the quarto text here and in ll. 58, 61, 68, and 96; the
Folio calls him a gentleman.) **put in** i.e., to harbor

CASSIO
  He's had most favorable and happy speed.
  Tempests themselves, high seas, and howling winds,
  The guttered rocks and congregated sands—   71
  Traitors ensteeped to clog the guiltless keel—   72
  As having sense of beauty, do omit   73
  Their mortal natures, letting go safely by   74
  The divine Desdemona.
MONTANO   What is she?
CASSIO
  She that I spake of, our great captain's captain,
  Left in the conduct of the bold Iago,
  Whose footing here anticipates our thoughts   78
  A sennight's speed. Great Jove, Othello guard,   79
  And swell his sail with thine own powerful breath,
  That he may bless this bay with his tall ship,   81
  Make love's quick pants in Desdemona's arms,
  Give renewed fire to our extinct spirits,
  And bring all Cyprus comfort!

        Enter Desdemona, Iago, Roderigo, and Emilia.

                          O, behold,
  The riches of the ship is come on shore!   [*He kneels.*]
  You men of Cyprus, let her have your knees.
  Hail to thee, lady! And the grace of heaven
  Before, behind thee, and on every hand
  Enwheel thee round!   [*He rises.*]
DESDEMONA   I thank you, valiant Cassio.
  What tidings can you tell me of my lord?
CASSIO
  He is not yet arrived, nor know I aught
  But that he's well and will be shortly here.
DESDEMONA
  O, but I fear—How lost you company?
CASSIO
  The great contention of the sea and skies
  Parted our fellowship.
                    (*Within*) "A sail, a sail!" [*A shot.*]
                    But hark. A sail!

71 guttered jagged, trenched **72 ensteeped** lying under water **73 As** as
if. **omit** forbear to exercise **74 mortal** deadly **78 footing** landing
79 sennight's week's **81 tall** splendid, gallant

SECOND GENTLEMAN
  They give their greeting to the citadel.
  This likewise is a friend.
CASSIO   See for the news.
                          [*Exit Second Gentleman.*]
  Good Ancient, you are welcome. [*Kissing Emilia.*]
    Welcome, mistress.
  Let it not gall your patience, good Iago,
  That I extend my manners. 'Tis my breeding   100
  That gives me this bold show of courtesy.
IAGO
  Sir, would she give you so much of her lips
  As of her tongue she oft bestows on me,
  You would have enough.
DESDEMONA   Alas, she has no speech!
IAGO   In faith, too much.
  I find it still, when I have list to sleep.   107
  Marry, before your ladyship, I grant,
  She puts her tongue a little in her heart
  And chides with thinking.
EMILIA   You have little cause to say so. 110
IAGO
  Come on, come on. You are pictures out of doors,   111
  Bells in your parlors, wildcats in your kitchens,   112
  Saints in your injuries, devils being offended,   113
  Players in your huswifery, and huswives in your beds. 114
DESDEMONA   O, fie upon thee, slanderer!
IAGO
  Nay, it is true, or else I am a Turk.
  You rise to play, and go to bed to work.
EMILIA
  You shall not write my praise.
IAGO   No, let me not.
DESDEMONA
  What wouldst write of me, if thou shouldst praise me?

---

100 extend show   **107 still** always.   **list** desire   **110 with thinking** i.e.,
in her thoughts only   **111 pictures out of doors** i.e., silent and well-
behaved in public   **112 Bells** i.e., jangling, noisy, and brazen.   **in your
kitchens** i.e., in domestic affairs. (Ladies would not do the cooking.)
113 Saints martyrs   **114 Players** idlers, triflers, or deceivers.   **huswifery** housekeeping.   **huswives** hussies (i.e., women are "busy" in bed, or
thrifty in dispensing sexual favors)

IAGO
O gentle lady, do not put me to 't,
For I am nothing if not critical.   121
DESDEMONA
Come on, assay.—There's one gone to the harbor?   122
IAGO   Ay, madam.
DESDEMONA
I am not merry, but I do beguile
The thing I am by seeming otherwise.   125
Come, how wouldst thou praise me?
IAGO
I am about it, but indeed my invention
Comes from my pate as birdlime does from frieze—   128
It plucks out brains and all. But my Muse labors,   129
And thus she is delivered:
If she be fair and wise, fairness and wit,
The one's for use, the other useth it.   132
DESDEMONA
Well praised! How if she be black and witty?   133
IAGO
If she be black, and thereto have a wit,
She'll find a white that shall her blackness fit.   135
DESDEMONA
Worse and worse.
EMILIA   How if fair and foolish?
IAGO
She never yet was foolish that was fair,
For even her folly helped her to an heir.   138
DESDEMONA   These are old fond paradoxes to make fools 139
laugh i' th' alehouse. What miserable praise hast thou
for her that's foul and foolish?   141
IAGO
There's none so foul and foolish thereunto,
But does foul pranks which fair and wise ones do.   143

121 **critical** censorious   122 **assay** try   125 **The thing I am** i.e., my
anxious self   128 **birdlime** sticky substance used to catch small birds.
frieze coarse woolen cloth   129 **labors** (1) exerts herself (2) prepares to
deliver a child (with a following pun on *delivered* in l. 130)   132 **The
one's . . . it** i.e., her cleverness will make use of her beauty   133 **black**
dark complexioned, brunette   135 **white** a fair person (with wordplay
on *wight*, a person).   **fit** (with sexual suggestion of mating)   138 **folly**
(with added meaning of "lechery, wantonness").   **to an heir** i.e., to bear
a child   139 **fond** foolish   141 **foul** ugly   143 **foul** sluttish

DESDEMONA O heavy ignorance! Thou praisest the worst
best. But what praise couldst thou bestow on a deserving woman indeed, one that, in the authority of her
merit, did justly put on the vouch of very malice itself? 147

IAGO

She that was ever fair, and never proud,
Had tongue at will, and yet was never loud,
Never lacked gold and yet went never gay,   150
Fled from her wish, and yet said, "Now I may,"   151
She that being angered, her revenge being nigh,
Bade her wrong stay and her displeasure fly,   153
She that in wisdom never was so frail
To change the cod's head for the salmon's tail,   155
She that could think and ne'er disclose her mind,
See suitors following and not look behind,
She was a wight, if ever such wight were—

DESDEMONA To do what?

IAGO

To suckle fools and chronicle small beer.   160

DESDEMONA O most lame and impotent conclusion! Do
not learn of him, Emilia, though he be thy husband.
How say you, Cassio? Is he not a most profane and   163
liberal counselor?   164

CASSIO He speaks home, madam. You may relish him   165
more in the soldier than in the scholar.   166

                    [Cassio and Desdemona stand together,
                              conversing intimately.]

IAGO [Aside] He takes her by the palm. Ay, well said,   167
whisper. With as little a web as this will I ensnare as
great a fly as Cassio. Ay, smile upon her, do; I will
gyve thee in thine own courtship. You say true; 'tis so,   170
indeed. If such tricks as these strip you out of your

147 put . . . vouch compel the approval 150 gay extravagantly
clothed 151 Fled . . . may avoided temptation where the choice was
hers 153 Bade . . . stay i.e., resolved to put up with her injury pa-
tiently 155 To . . . tail i.e., to exchange a lackluster husband for a
sexy lover (?) (Cod's head is slang for penis, and tail for pudendum.)
160 suckle fools breastfeed babies. chronicle small beer i.e., keep petty
household accounts, keep track of trivial matters 163 profane irrever-
ent, ribald 164 liberal licentious, free-spoken 165 home i.e., without
reserve. relish appreciate 166 in in the character of 167 well said
well done 170 gyve fetter, shackle. courtship courtesy, show of
courtly manners

lieutenantry, it had been better you had not kissed
your three fingers so oft, which now again you are
most apt to play the sir in. Very good; well kissed! An   174
excellent courtesy! 'Tis so, indeed. Yet again your fingers
to your lips? Would they were clyster pipes for your   176
sake! [*Trumpet within.*] The Moor! I know his trumpet.

CASSIO   'Tis truly so.

DESDEMONA   Let's meet him and receive him.

CASSIO   Lo, where he comes!

     Enter Othello and attendants.

OTHELLO
  O my fair warrior!

DESDEMONA   My dear Othello!

OTHELLO
  It gives me wonder great as my content
  To see you here before me. O my soul's joy!
  If after every tempest come such calms,
  May the winds blow till they have wakened death!
  And let the laboring bark climb hills of seas
  Olympus-high, and duck again as low
  As hell's from heaven! If it were now to die,
  'Twere now to be most happy, for I fear
  My soul hath her content so absolute
  That not another comfort like to this
  Succeeds in unknown fate.

DESDEMONA   The heavens forbid   192
  But that our loves and comforts should increase
  Even as our days do grow!

OTHELLO   Amen to that, sweet powers!
  I cannot speak enough of this content.
  It stops me here; it is too much of joy.
  And this, and this, the greatest discords be   198

                              [*They kiss*]

  That e'er our hearts shall make!

IAGO [*Aside*]   O, you are well tuned now!

---

174 the sir i.e., the fine gentleman   **176 clyster pipes** tubes used for
enemas and douches   **192 Succeeds . . . fate** i.e., can follow in the
unknown future   **198 s.d. They kiss** (The direction is from the
quarto.)

But I'll set down the pegs that make this music,　201
As honest as I am.
OTHELLO　Come, let us to the castle.
　News, friends! Our wars are done, the Turks are
　　drowned.
　How does my old acquaintance of this isle?—
　Honey, you shall be well desired in Cyprus;　206
　I have found great love amongst them. O my sweet,
　I prattle out of fashion, and I dote　208
　In mine own comforts.—I prithee, good Iago,
　Go to the bay and disembark my coffers.　210
　Bring thou the master to the citadel;　211
　He is a good one, and his worthiness
　Does challenge much respect.—Come, Desdemona.—　213
　Once more, well met at Cyprus!
　　　　　　Exeunt Othello and Desdemona [and all
　　　　　　　　　　　　but Iago and Roderigo].
IAGO [*To an attendant*]　Do thou meet me presently at
　the harbor. [*To Roderigo*.] Come hither. If thou be'st
　valiant—as, they say, base men being in love have　217
　then a nobility in their natures more than is native to
　them—list me. The Lieutenant tonight watches on the　219
　court of guard. First, I must tell thee this: Desdemona　220
　is directly in love with him.
RODERIGO　With him? Why, 'tis not possible.
IAGO　Lay thy finger thus, and let thy soul be instructed.　223
　Mark me with what violence she first loved the Moor,
　but for bragging and telling her fantastical lies.　225
　To love him still for prating? Let not thy discreet
　heart think it. Her eye must be fed; and what delight
　shall she have to look on the devil? When the blood is
　made dull with the act of sport, there should be, again
　to inflame it and to give satiety a fresh appetite, love-
　liness in favor, sympathy in years, manners, and　231

201 set down loosen (and hence untune the instrument)　**206 desired**
welcomed　**208 out of fashion** irrelevantly (?)　**210 coffers** chests,
baggage　**211 master** ship's captain　**213 challenge** lay claim to, deserve　**217 base men** even lowly born men　**219 list** listen to　**220 court
of guard** guardhouse. (Cassio is in charge of the watch.)　**223 thus** i.e.,
on your lips　**225 but** only　**231 favor** appearance.　**sympathy** corre-
spondence, similarity

beauties—all which the Moor is defective in. Now, for
want of these required conveniences, her delicate ten- 233
derness will find itself abused, begin to heave the 234
gorge, disrelish and abhor the Moor. Very nature will 235
instruct her in it and compel her to some second
choice. Now, sir, this granted—as it is a most preg- 237
nant and unforced position—who stands so eminent 238
in the degree of this fortune as Cassio does? A knave
very voluble, no further conscionable than in putting 240
on the mere form of civil and humane seeming for the 241
better compassing of his salt and most hidden loose 242
affection. Why, none, why, none. A slipper and subtle 243
knave, a finder out of occasions, that has an eye can 244
stamp and counterfeit advantages, though true advantage 245
never present itself; a devilish knave. Besides, the
knave is handsome, young, and hath all those requi-
sites in him that folly and green minds look after. A 248
pestilent complete knave, and the woman hath found 249
him already.   250

RODERIGO I cannot believe that in her. She's full of most
    blessed condition.   252

IAGO Blessed fig's end! The wine she drinks is made of 253
    grapes. If she had been blessed, she would never have
    loved the Moor. Blessed pudding! Didst thou not see 255
    her paddle with the palm of his hand? Didst not mark
    that?

RODERIGO Yes, that I did; but that was but courtesy.

IAGO Lechery, by this hand. An index and obscure pro- 259
    logue to the history of lust and foul thoughts. They
    met so near with their lips that their breaths embraced
    together. Villainous thoughts, Roderigo! When these
    mutualities so marshal the way, hard at hand comes 263

233 **conveniences** compatibilities   **234–235 heave the gorge** experience
nausea   **237–238 pregnant** evident, cogent   **240 conscionable** conscien-
tious, conscience-bound   **241 humane** polite, courteous   **242 salt**
licentious   **243 affection** passion.   **slipper** slippery   **244–245 an eye
can stamp** an eye that can coin, create   **245 advantages** favorable
opportunities   **248 folly** wantonness.   **green** immature   **249–250 found
him** sized him up   **252 condition** disposition   **253 fig's end** (See 1.3.322
for the vulgar gesture of the fig.)   **255 pudding** sausage   **259 index**
table of contents.   **obscure** (i.e., the *lust and foul thoughts*, l. 260, are
secret, hidden from view)   **263 mutualities** exchanges, intimacies.
hard at hand closely following

the master and main exercise, th' incorporate conclu- 264
sion. Pish! But, sir, be you ruled by me. I have brought
you from Venice. Watch you tonight; for the com- 266
mand, I'll lay 't upon you. Cassio knows you not. I'll 267
not be far from you. Do you find some occasion to
anger Cassio, either by speaking too loud, or tainting 269
his discipline, or from what other course you please,
which the time shall more favorably minister. 271

RODERIGO Well.

IAGO Sir, he's rash and very sudden in choler, and hap- 273
ly may strike at you. Provoke him that he may, for 274
even out of that will I cause these of Cyprus to mutiny, 275
whose qualification shall come into no true taste again 276
but by the displanting of Cassio. So shall you have a
shorter journey to your desires by the means I shall
then have to prefer them, and the impediment most 279
profitably removed, without the which there were no
expectation of our prosperity.

RODERIGO I will do this, if you can bring it to any
opportunity.

IAGO I warrant thee. Meet me by and by at the citadel. 284
I must fetch his necessaries ashore. Farewell.

RODERIGO Adieu. *Exit.*

IAGO
That Cassio loves her, I do well believe 't;
That she loves him, 'tis apt and of great credit. 288
The Moor, howbeit that I endure him not,
Is of a constant, loving, noble nature,
And I dare think he'll prove to Desdemona
A most dear husband. Now, I do love her too,
Not out of absolute lust—though peradventure
I stand accountant for as great a sin— 294
But partly led to diet my revenge 295
For that I do suspect the lusty Moor
Hath leaped into my seat, the thought whereof

---

264 **incorporate** carnal   266 **Watch you** stand watch   266–267 **for the command . . . you** I'll arrange for you to be appointed, given orders
269 **tainting** disparaging   271 **minister** provide   273 **choler** wrath
273–274 **haply** perhaps   275 **mutiny** riot   276 **qualification** appeasement.   **true taste** acceptable state   279 **prefer** advance   284 **warrant** assure.   **by and by** immediately   288 **apt** probable.   **credit** credibility   294 **accountant** accountable   295 **diet** feed

Doth, like a poisonous mineral, gnaw my innards;
And nothing can or shall content my soul
Till I am evened with him, wife for wife,
Or failing so, yet that I put the Moor
At least into a jealousy so strong
That judgment cannot cure. Which thing to do,
If this poor trash of Venice, whom I trace   304
For his quick hunting, stand the putting on,   305
I'll have our Michael Cassio on the hip,   306
Abuse him to the Moor in the rank garb—   307
For I fear Cassio with my nightcap too—   308
Make the Moor thank me, love me, and reward me
For making him egregiously an ass
And practicing upon his peace and quiet   311
Even to madness. 'Tis here, but yet confused.
Knavery's plain face is never seen till used.   *Exit.*

2.2   *Enter Othello's Herald with a proclamation.*

HERALD   It is Othello's pleasure, our noble and valiant
general, that, upon certain tidings now arrived, im-
porting the mere perdition of the Turkish fleet, every 3
man put himself into triumph: some to dance, some
to make bonfires, each man to what sport and revels
his addiction leads him. For, besides these beneficial 6
news, it is the celebration of his nuptial. So much was
his pleasure should be proclaimed. All offices are open, 8
and there is full liberty of feasting from this present
hour of five till the bell have told eleven. Heaven bless
the isle of Cyprus and our noble general Othello!
                                                    Exit.

✤

304 **trace** i.e., train, or follow (?), or perhaps *trash*, a hunting term,
meaning to put weights on a hunting dog in order to slow him down
305 **For** to make more eager.   **stand . . . on** respond properly when I
incite him to quarrel   306 **on the hip** at my mercy, where I can throw
him. (A wrestling term.)   307 **Abuse** slander.   **rank garb** coarse manner,
gross fashion   308 **with my nightcap** i.e., as a rival in my bed, as one
who gives me cuckold's horns   311 **practicing upon** plotting against

2.2. Location: Cyprus. A street.
3 **mere perdition** complete destruction   6 **addiction** inclination
8 **offices** rooms where food and drink are kept

2.3   *Enter Othello, Desdemona, Cassio, and attendants.*

OTHELLO
Good Michael, look you to the guard tonight.
Let's teach ourselves that honorable stop   2
Not to outsport discretion.   3
CASSIO
Iago hath direction what to do,
But notwithstanding, with my personal eye
Will I look to 't.
OTHELLO   Iago is most honest.
Michael, good night. Tomorrow with your earliest   7
Let me have speech with you. [*To Desdemona.*] Come,
    my dear love,
The purchase made, the fruits are to ensue;   9
That profit's yet to come 'tween me and you.—   10
Good night.
        Exit [Othello, with Desdemona and attendants].

        Enter Iago.

CASSIO Welcome, Iago. We must to the watch.
IAGO Not this hour, Lieutenant; 'tis not yet ten o' the 13
clock. Our general cast us thus early for the love of his 14
Desdemona; who let us not therefore blame. He hath 15
not yet made wanton the night with her, and she is
sport for Jove.
CASSIO She's a most exquisite lady.
IAGO And, I'll warrant her, full of game.
CASSIO Indeed, she's a most fresh and delicate creature.
IAGO What an eye she has! Methinks it sounds a parley 21
to provocation.
CASSIO An inviting eye, and yet methinks right modest.
IAGO And when she speaks, is it not an alarum to love? 24

2.3. Location: Cyprus. The citadel.
2 stop restraint   **3 outsport** celebrate beyond the bounds of   **7 with
your earliest** at your earliest convenience   **9–10 The purchase . . . you**
i.e., though married, we haven't yet consummated our love   **13 Not this
hour** not for an hour yet   **14 cast** dismissed   **15 who** i.e., Othello
21 sounds a parley calls for a conference, issues an invitation
24 alarum signal calling men to arms (continuing the military metaphor
of *parley*, l. 21)

CASSIO She is indeed perfection.

IAGO Well, happiness to their sheets! Come, Lieutenant,
I have a stoup of wine, and here without are a brace 27
of Cyprus gallants that would fain have a measure to 28
the health of black Othello.

CASSIO Not tonight, good Iago. I have very poor and
unhappy brains for drinking. I could well wish courtesy would invent some other custom of entertainment.

IAGO O, they are our friends. But one cup! I'll drink
for you.   35

CASSIO I have drunk but one cup tonight, and that was
craftily qualified too, and behold what innovation it 37
makes here. I am unfortunate in the infirmity and 38
dare not task my weakness with any more.

IAGO What, man? 'Tis a night of revels. The gallants
desire it.

CASSIO Where are they?

IAGO Here at the door. I pray you, call them in.

CASSIO I'll do 't, but it dislikes me.   *Exit.* 44

IAGO
If I can fasten but one cup upon him,
With that which he hath drunk tonight already,
He'll be as full of quarrel and offense
As my young mistress' dog. Now, my sick fool Roderigo,
Whom love hath turned almost the wrong side out,
To Desdemona hath tonight caroused   50
Potations pottle-deep; and he's to watch.   51
Three lads of Cyprus—noble swelling spirits,   52
That hold their honors in a wary distance,   53
The very elements of this warlike isle—   54
Have I tonight flustered with flowing cups,
And they watch too. Now, 'mongst this flock of
    drunkards   56

27 **stoup** measure of liquor, two quarts. **without** outside. **brace** pair
28 **have a measure** drink a toast 35 **for you** in your place. (Iago will do
the steady drinking to keep the gallants company while Cassio has only
one cup.) 37 **qualified** diluted. **innovation** disturbance, insurrection
38 **here** i.e., in my head 44 **dislikes** displeases 50 **caroused** drunk
off 51 **pottle-deep** to the bottom of the tankard 52 **swelling** proud
53 **hold . . . distance** i.e., are extremely sensitive of their honor 54 **very
elements** true representatives 56 **watch** are members of the guard

Am I to put our Cassio in some action
That may offend the isle.—But here they come.

*Enter Cassio, Montano, and gentlemen; [servants
following with wine].*

If consequence do but approve my dream,   59
My boat sails freely both with wind and stream.   60
CASSIO   'Fore God, they have given me a rouse already.   61
MONTANO   Good faith, a little one; not past a pint, as I
am a soldier.
IAGO   Some wine, ho!

[*Sings.*] "And let me the cannikin clink, clink,   65
     And let me the cannikin clink.
        A soldier's a man,
        O, man's life's but a span;   68
     Why, then, let a soldier drink."

Some wine, boys!
CASSIO   'Fore God, an excellent song.
IAGO   I learned it in England, where indeed they are
most potent in potting. Your Dane, your German, and   73
your swag-bellied Hollander—drink, ho!—are noth-
ing to your English.
CASSIO   Is your Englishman so exquisite in his drinking?
IAGO   Why, he drinks you, with facility, your Dane   77
dead drunk; he sweats not to overthrow your Almain;   78
he gives your Hollander a vomit ere the next pottle can
be filled.
CASSIO   To the health of our general!
MONTANO   I am for it, Lieutenant, and I'll do you justice.   82
IAGO   O sweet England! [*Sings.*]

     "King Stephen was and-a worthy peer,
        His breeches cost him but a crown;
     He held them sixpence all too dear;
        With that he called the tailor lown.   87

59 If . . . dream if subsequent events will only substantiate my
scheme   60 stream current   61 rouse full draft of liquor   65 cannikin
small drinking vessel   68 span i.e., brief span of time. (Compare Psalm
39:5 as rendered in the Book of Common Prayer: "Thou hast made my
days as it were a span long.")   73 potting drinking   77 drinks you
drinks.   your Dane your typical Dane   78 Almain German   82 I'll . . .
justice i.e., I'll drink as much as you   87 lown lout, rascal

He was a wight of high renown,
  And thou art but of low degree.
    'Tis pride that pulls the country down;   90
      Then take thy auld cloak about thee."   91

Some wine, ho!

CASSIO 'Fore God, this is a more exquisite song than
the other.

IAGO Will you hear 't again?

CASSIO No, for I hold him to be unworthy of his place
that does those things. Well, God's above all; and
there be souls must be saved, and there be souls must
not be saved.

IAGO It's true, good Lieutenant.

CASSIO For mine own part—no offense to the General,
nor any man of quality—I hope to be saved.   102

IAGO And so do I too, Lieutenant.

CASSIO Ay, but, by your leave, not before me. The lieutenant is to be saved before the ancient. Let's have no
more of this. Let's to our affairs. God forgive us our
sins! Gentlemen, let's look to our business. Do not
think, gentlemen, I am drunk. This is my ancient; this
is my right hand, and this is my left. I am not drunk
now. I can stand well enough, and speak well enough.

GENTLEMEN Excellent well.

CASSIO Why, very well then. You must not think then
that I am drunk.   *Exit.*

MONTANO
To th' platform, masters. Come, let's set the watch. 114
                              [*Exeunt Gentlemen.*]

IAGO
You see this fellow that is gone before.
He's a soldier fit to stand by Caesar
And give direction; and do but see his vice.
'Tis to his virtue a just equinox,   118
The one as long as th' other. 'Tis pity of him.
I fear the trust Othello puts him in,
On some odd time of his infirmity,
Will shake this island.

---

90 pride i.e., extravagance in dress **91 auld** old **102 quality** rank
114 set the watch mount the guard **118 just equinox** exact counterpart.
(*Equinox* is an equal length of days and nights.)

MONTANO   But is he often thus?

IAGO
  'Tis evermore the prologue to his sleep.
  He'll watch the horologe a double set,   124
  If drink rock not his cradle.

MONTANO   It were well
  The General were put in mind of it.
  Perhaps he sees it not, or his good nature
  Prizes the virtue that appears in Cassio
  And looks not on his evils. Is not this true?

     Enter Roderigo.

IAGO [*Aside to him*]   How now, Roderigo?
  I pray you, after the Lieutenant; go.   [*Exit Roderigo.*]

MONTANO
  And 'tis great pity that the noble Moor
  Should hazard such a place as his own second   133
  With one of an engraffed infirmity.   134
  It were an honest action to say so
  To the Moor.

IAGO   Not I, for this fair island.
  I do love Cassio well and would do much
  To cure him of this evil.   [*Cry within:* "Help! Help!"]
                 But hark! What noise?   138

     Enter Cassio, pursuing Roderigo.

CASSIO   Zounds, you rogue! You rascal!

MONTANO   What's the matter, Lieutenant?

CASSIO   A knave teach me my duty? I'll beat the knave
  into a twiggen bottle.   142

RODERIGO   Beat me?

CASSIO   Dost thou prate, rogue?   [*He strikes Roderigo.*]

MONTANO   Nay, good Lieutenant. [*Staying him.*] I pray
  you, sir, hold your hand.

CASSIO   Let me go, sir, or I'll knock you o'er the maz- 147
ard.   148

---

124 watch ... set stay awake twice around the clock or *horologe*
133–134 hazard ... With risk giving such an important position as his
second in command to **134 engraffed** engrafted, inveterate **138 s.d.
pursuing** (The quarto text reads, "driving in.") **142 twiggen** wicker-
covered. (Cassio vows to assail Roderigo until his skin resembles
wickerwork, or until he has driven Roderigo through the holes in a
wickerwork.) **147–148 mazard** i.e., head. (Literally, a drinking vessel.)

MONTANO   Come, come, you're drunk.
CASSIO   Drunk?   [*They fight.*]
IAGO [*Aside to Roderigo*]
  Away, I say. Go out and cry a mutiny. [*Exit Roderigo.*] 151
  Nay, good Lieutenant—God's will, gentlemen—
  Help, ho!—Lieutenant—sir—Montano—sir—
  Help, masters!—Here's a goodly watch indeed!   154
                                          [*A bell rings.*]
  Who's that which rings the bell?—Diablo, ho!   155
  The town will rise. God's will, Lieutenant, hold!   156
  You'll be ashamed forever.

      Enter Othello and attendants [*with weapons*].

OTHELLO
  What is the matter here?
MONTANO   Zounds, I bleed still.
  I am hurt to th' death. He dies! [*He thrusts at Cassio.*]
OTHELLO   Hold, for your lives!
IAGO
  Hold, ho! Lieutenant—sir—Montano—gentlemen—
  Have you forgot all sense of place and duty?
  Hold! The General speaks to you. Hold, for shame!
OTHELLO
  Why, how now, ho! From whence ariseth this?
  Are we turned Turks, and to ourselves do that
  Which heaven hath forbid the Ottomites?   165
  For Christian shame, put by this barbarous brawl!
  He that stirs next to carve for his own rage   167
  Holds his soul light; he dies upon his motion.   168
  Silence that dreadful bell. It frights the isle
  From her propriety. What is the matter, masters?   170
  Honest Iago, that looks dead with grieving,
  Speak. Who began this? On thy love, I charge thee.
IAGO
  I do not know. Friends all but now, even now,

151 **mutiny** riot   154 **masters** sirs   **s.d. A bell rings** (This direction is
from the quarto, as are *Exit Roderigo* at l. 131, *They fight* at l. 150, and
with weapons at l. 157.)   155 **Diablo** the devil   156 **rise** grow riotous
165 **forbid** i.e., prevented, by destroying their fleet, so that the Venetians
need not fight them   167 **carve for** i.e., indulge, satisfy   168 **Holds . . .
light** i.e., places little value on his life.   **upon his motion** if he moves
170 **propriety** proper state or condition

In quarter and in terms like bride and groom 174
Devesting them for bed; and then, but now— 175
As if some planet had unwitted men—
Swords out, and tilting one at other's breast
In opposition bloody. I cannot speak 178
Any beginning to this peevish odds; 179
And would in action glorious I had lost
Those legs that brought me to a part of it!

OTHELLO
How comes it, Michael, you are thus forgot? 182

CASSIO
I pray you, pardon me. I cannot speak.

OTHELLO
Worthy Montano, you were wont be civil; 184
The gravity and stillness of your youth 185
The world hath noted, and your name is great
In mouths of wisest censure. What's the matter 187
That you unlace your reputation thus 188
And spend your rich opinion for the name 189
Of a night-brawler? Give me answer to it.

MONTANO
Worthy Othello, I am hurt to danger.
Your officer, Iago, can inform you—
While I spare speech, which something now offends
  me— 193
Of all that I do know; nor know I aught
By me that's said or done amiss this night,
Unless self-charity be sometimes a vice,
And to defend ourselves it be a sin
When violence assails us.

OTHELLO   Now, by heaven,
My blood begins my safer guides to rule, 199
And passion, having my best judgment collied, 200

---

174 In quarter in friendly conduct, within bounds. **in terms** on good terms **175 Devesting them** undressing themselves **178 speak** explain **179 peevish odds** childish quarrel **182 are thus forgot** have forgotten yourself thus **184 wont be** accustomed to be **185 stillness** sobriety **187 censure** judgment **188 unlace** undo, lay open (as one might loose the strings of a purse containing reputation) **189 opinion** reputation **193 something** somewhat. **offends** pains **199 blood** passion (of anger). **guides** i.e., reason **200 collied** darkened

Assays to lead the way. Zounds, if I stir,   201
Or do but lift this arm, the best of you
Shall sink in my rebuke. Give me to know
How this foul rout began, who set it on;   204
And he that is approved in this offense,   205
Though he had twinned with me, both at a birth,
Shall lose me. What? In a town of war
Yet wild, the people's hearts brim full of fear,
To manage private and domestic quarrel?   209
In night, and on the court and guard of safety?   210
'Tis monstrous. Iago, who began 't?

MONTANO [*To Iago*]
If partially affined, or leagued in office,   212
Thou dost deliver more or less than truth,
Thou art no soldier.

IAGO   Touch me not so near.
I had rather have this tongue cut from my mouth
Than it should do offense to Michael Cassio;
Yet, I persuade myself, to speak the truth
Shall nothing wrong him. Thus it is, General.
Montano and myself being in speech,
There comes a fellow crying out for help,
And Cassio following him with determined sword
To execute upon him. Sir, this gentleman   222
                              [*Indicating Montano*]
Steps in to Cassio and entreats his pause.
Myself the crying fellow did pursue,
Lest by his clamor—as it so fell out—
The town might fall in fright. He, swift of foot,
Outran my purpose, and I returned, the rather   227
For that I heard the clink and fall of swords
And Cassio high in oath, which till tonight
I ne'er might say before. When I came back—
For this was brief—I found them close together
At blow and thrust, even as again they were

---

201 Assays undertakes   **204 rout** riot   **205 approved in** found guilty of
209 manage undertake   **210 on . . . safety** at the main guardhouse or head-
quarters and on watch   **212 partially affined** made partial by some personal
relationship.   **leagued in office** in league as fellow officers   **222 execute**
give effect to (his anger)   **227 rather** sooner

When you yourself did part them.
More of this matter cannot I report.
But men are men; the best sometimes forget.   235
Though Cassio did some little wrong to him,
As men in rage strike those that wish them best,   237
Yet surely Cassio, I believe, received
From him that fled some strange indignity,
Which patience could not pass.

OTHELLO   I know, Iago,   240
Thy honesty and love doth mince this matter,
Making it light to Cassio. Cassio, I love thee,
But nevermore be officer of mine.

    Enter Desdemona, attended.

Look if my gentle love be not raised up.
I'll make thee an example.

DESDEMONA
What is the matter, dear?

OTHELLO   All's well now, sweeting;
Come away to bed. [*To Montano.*] Sir, for your hurts,
Myself will be your surgeon.—Lead him off.   248

                     [*Montano is led off.*]

Iago, look with care about the town
And silence those whom this vile brawl distracted.
Come, Desdemona. 'Tis the soldiers' life
To have their balmy slumbers waked with strife.

            Exit [*with all but Iago and Cassio*].

IAGO What, are you hurt, Lieutenant?

CASSIO Ay, past all surgery.

IAGO Marry, God forbid!

CASSIO Reputation, reputation, reputation! O, I have
lost my reputation! I have lost the immortal part of
myself, and what remains is bestial. My reputation,
Iago, my reputation!

IAGO As I am an honest man, I thought you had received some bodily wound; there is more sense in that
than in reputation. Reputation is an idle and most

235 forget forget themselves   **237 those . . . best** i.e., even those who are
well disposed   **240 pass** pass over, overlook   **248 be your surgeon** i.e.,
make sure you receive medical attention

false imposition, oft got without merit and lost with- 263
out deserving. You have lost no reputation at all, unless you repute yourself such a loser. What, man, there
are ways to recover the General again. You are but now 266
cast in his mood—a punishment more in policy than in 267
malice, even so as one would beat his offenseless dog 268
to affright an imperious lion. Sue to him again and 269
he's yours.

CASSIO I will rather sue to be despised than to deceive
so good a commander with so slight, so drunken, and 272
so indiscreet an officer. Drunk? And speak parrot? 273
And squabble? Swagger? Swear? And discourse fustian with one's own shadow? O thou invisible spirit
of wine, if thou hast no name to be known by, let us
call thee devil!

IAGO What was he that you followed with your sword?
What had he done to you?

CASSIO I know not.

IAGO Is 't possible?

CASSIO I remember a mass of things, but nothing distinctly; a quarrel, but nothing wherefore. O God, that 283
men should put an enemy in their mouths to steal
away their brains! That we should, with joy, pleas-
ance, revel, and applause transform ourselves into
beasts!

IAGO Why, but you are now well enough. How came
you thus recovered?

CASSIO It hath pleased the devil drunkenness to give
place to the devil wrath. One unperfectness shows me
another, to make me frankly despise myself.

IAGO Come, you are too severe a moraler. As the time, 293
the place, and the condition of this country stands, I
could heartily wish this had not befallen; but since it is

---

263 imposition thing artificially imposed and of no real value   **266 recover** regain favor with   **267 cast in his mood** dismissed in a moment
of anger.   **in policy** done for expediency's sake and as a public gesture
268–269 would . . . lion i.e., would make an example of a minor offender
in order to deter more important and dangerous offenders   **269 Sue** petition   **272 slight** worthless   **273 speak parrot** talk nonsense, rant. (*Discourse
fustian*, ll. 274–275, has much the same meaning.)   **283 wherefore** why
293 moraler moralizer

as it is, mend it for your own good.

CASSIO I will ask him for my place again; he shall tell
me I am a drunkard! Had I as many mouths as Hydra, 298
such an answer would stop them all. To be now a sen-
sible man, by and by a fool, and presently a beast! O,
strange! Every inordinate cup is unblessed, and the ingredient is a devil.

IAGO Come, come, good wine is a good familiar creature, if it be well used. Exclaim no more against it.
And, good Lieutenant, I think you think I love you.

CASSIO I have well approved it, sir. I drunk! 306

IAGO You or any man living may be drunk at a time, 307
man. I'll tell you what you shall do. Our general's wife
is now the general—I may say so in this respect, for 309
that he hath devoted and given up himself to the con- 310
templation, mark, and denotement of her parts and 311
graces. Confess yourself freely to her; importune her
help to put you in your place again. She is of so free, 313
so kind, so apt, so blessed a disposition, she holds it a
vice in her goodness not to do more than she is re-
quested. This broken joint between you and her husband entreat her to splinter; and, my fortunes against 317
any lay worth naming, this crack of your love shall 318
grow stronger than it was before.

CASSIO You advise me well.

IAGO I protest, in the sincerity of love and honest kind- 321
ness.

CASSIO I think it freely; and betimes in the morning I 323
will beseech the virtuous Desdemona to undertake for
me. I am desperate of my fortunes if they check me 325
here.

IAGO You are in the right. Good night, Lieutenant. I
must to the watch.

---

298 Hydra the Lernaean Hydra, a monster with many heads and the
ability to grow two heads when one was cut off; slain by Hercules as
the second of his twelve labors **306 approved** proved **307 at a time** at
one time or another **309–310 in . . . that** in view of this fact, that
311 mark, and denotement (Both words mean "observation.") **parts**
qualities **313 free** generous **317 splinter** bind with splints **318 lay**
stake, wager **321 protest** insist, declare **323 freely** unreservedly
325 check repulse

CASSIO Good night, honest Iago.   *Exit Cassio.*

IAGO

And what's he then that says I play the villain,
When this advice is free I give and honest,   331
Probal to thinking, and indeed the course   332
To win the Moor again? For 'tis most easy
Th' inclining Desdemona to subdue   334
In any honest suit; she's framed as fruitful   335
As the free elements. And then for her   336
To win the Moor—were 't to renounce his baptism,
All seals and symbols of redeemèd sin—
His soul is so enfettered to her love
That she may make, unmake, do what she list,
Even as her appetite shall play the god
With his weak function. How am I then a villain,   342
To counsel Cassio to this parallel course   343
Directly to his good? Divinity of hell!   344
When devils will the blackest sins put on,   345
They do suggest at first with heavenly shows,   346
As I do now. For whiles this honest fool
Plies Desdemona to repair his fortune,
And she for him pleads strongly to the Moor,
I'll pour this pestilence into his ear,
That she repeals him for her body's lust;   351
And by how much she strives to do him good,
She shall undo her credit with the Moor.
So will I turn her virtue into pitch,
And out of her own goodness make the net
That shall enmesh them all.

Enter Roderigo.

                              How now, Roderigo?
RODERIGO I do follow here in the chase, not like a

---

331 free (1) free from guile (2) freely given   **332 Probal** probable, reason-
able   **334 inclining** favorably disposed.   **subdue** persuade   **335 fruitful**
generous   **336 free elements** i.e., earth, air, fire, and water, which
sustain life (?)   **342 function** exercise of faculties (weakened by his
fondness for her)   **343 parallel** corresponding to these facts and to his
best interests   **344 Divinity of hell** inverted theology of hell (which
seduces the soul to its damnation)   **345 put on** further, instigate
346 suggest tempt   **351 repeals him** i.e., attempts to get him restored

hound that hunts, but one that fills up the cry. My 358
money is almost spent; I have been tonight exceedingly well cudgeled; and I think the issue will be I
shall have so much experience for my pains, and so, 361
with no money at all and a little more wit, return again
to Venice.

IAGO
How poor are they that have not patience!
What wound did ever heal but by degrees?
Thou know'st we work by wit, and not by witchcraft,
And wit depends on dilatory time.
Does 't not go well? Cassio hath beaten thee,
And thou, by that small hurt, hast cashiered Cassio. 369
Though other things grow fair against the sun, 370
Yet fruits that blossom first will first be ripe. 371
Content thyself awhile. By the Mass, 'tis morning!
Pleasure and action make the hours seem short.
Retire thee; go where thou art billeted.
Away, I say! Thou shalt know more hereafter.
Nay, get thee gone.　　　　　　　　　*Exit Roderigo.*
　　　　　　　　Two things are to be done.
My wife must move for Cassio to her mistress; 377
I'll set her on;
Myself the while to draw the Moor apart
And bring him jump when he may Cassio find 380
Soliciting his wife. Ay, that's the way.
Dull not device by coldness and delay.　　　*Exit.* 382

❖

358 fills up the cry merely takes part as one of the pack　361 so
much just so much and no more　369 cashiered dismissed from service
370–371 Though . . . ripe i.e., the first part of our plan has already ripened
to fruition, and other parts are maturing in their own good time　377 move
plead　380 jump precisely　382 device plot.　coldness lack of zeal

3.1   *Enter Cassio [and] Musicians.*

CASSIO

Masters, play here—I will content your pains—   1
Something that's brief, and bid "Good morrow,
   General."   [*They play.*]

   [*Enter*] *Clown.*

CLOWN   Why, masters, have your instruments been in
   Naples, that they speak i' the nose thus?   4

A MUSICIAN   How, sir, how?

CLOWN   Are these, I pray you, wind instruments?

A MUSICIAN   Ay, marry, are they, sir.

CLOWN   O, thereby hangs a tail.

A MUSICIAN   Whereby hangs a tale, sir?

CLOWN   Marry, sir, by many a wind instrument that I   10
   know. But, masters, here's money for you. [*He gives
   money.*] And the General so likes your music that he
   desires you, for love's sake, to make no more noise   13
   with it.

A MUSICIAN   Well, sir, we will not.

CLOWN   If you have any music that may not be heard,   16
   to 't again; but, as they say, to hear music the General
   does not greatly care.

A MUSICIAN   We have none such, sir.

CLOWN   Then put up your pipes in your bag, for I'll   20
   away. Go, vanish into air, away!   *Exeunt Musicians.*   21

CASSIO   Dost thou hear, mine honest friend?

CLOWN   No, I hear not your honest friend; I hear you.

CASSIO   Prithee, keep up thy quillets. There's a poor   24
   piece of gold for thee. [*He gives money.*] If the gentlewoman that attends the General's wife be stirring, tell

---

3.1. Location: Before the chamber of Othello and Desdemona.
1 content reward.   **pains** efforts   **4 speak i' the nose** (1) sound nasal
(2) sound like one whose nose has been attacked by syphilis. (Naples
was popularly supposed to have a high incidence of venereal disease.)
10 wind instrument (With a joke on flatulence. The *tail,* l. 8, that hangs
nearby the *wind instrument* suggests the penis.)   **13 for love's sake**
(1) out of friendship and affection (2) for the sake of lovemaking in
Othello's marriage   **16 may not** cannot   **20–21 I'll away** (Possibly a
misprint, or a snatch of song?)   **24 keep up** do not bring out, do not
use.   **quillets** quibbles, puns

her there's one Cassio entreats her a little favor of 27
speech. Wilt thou do this? 28

CLOWN   She is stirring, sir. If she will stir hither, I shall
seem to notify unto her. 30

CASSIO
Do, good my friend.   *Exit Clown.*

     Enter Iago.

            In happy time, Iago. 31

IAGO   You have not been abed, then?

CASSIO   Why, no. The day had broke
Before we parted. I have made bold, Iago,
To send in to your wife. My suit to her
Is that she will to virtuous Desdemona
Procure me some access.

IAGO   I'll send her to you presently;
And I'll devise a means to draw the Moor
Out of the way, that your converse and business
May be more free.

CASSIO
I humbly thank you for 't.   *Exit [Iago].*
            I never knew
A Florentine more kind and honest. 43

     Enter Emilia.

EMILIA
Good morrow, good Lieutenant. I am sorry
For your displeasure; but all will sure be well. 45
The General and his wife are talking of it,
And she speaks for you stoutly. The Moor replies
That he you hurt is of great fame in Cyprus
And great affinity, and that in wholesome wisdom 49
He might not but refuse you; but he protests he loves you
And needs no other suitor but his likings
To take the safest occasion by the front 52
To bring you in again.

CASSIO   Yet I beseech you,

27–28 a little . . . speech the favor of a brief talk   **30 seem** deem it
good, think fit   **31 In happy time** i.e., well met   **43 Florentine** i.e.,
even a fellow Florentine. (Iago is a Venetian, Cassio a Florentine.)
45 displeasure fall from favor   **49 affinity** kindred, family connection
52 occasion . . . front opportunity by the forelock

If you think fit, or that it may be done,
Give me advantage of some brief discourse
With Desdemon alone.
EMILIA   Pray you, come in.
I will bestow you where you shall have time
To speak your bosom freely.   58
CASSIO   I am much bound to you.   [*Exeunt.*]

❖

3.2   *Enter Othello, Iago, and Gentlemen.*

OTHELLO [*Giving letters*]
These letters give, Iago, to the pilot,
And by him do my duties to the Senate.   2
That done, I will be walking on the works;   3
Repair there to me.
IAGO   Well, my good lord, I'll do 't.   4
OTHELLO
This fortification, gentlemen, shall we see 't?
GENTLEMEN   We'll wait upon your lordship.   *Exeunt.* 6

❖

3.3   *Enter Desdemona, Cassio, and Emilia.*

DESDEMONA
Be thou assured, good Cassio, I will do
All my abilities in thy behalf.
EMILIA
Good madam, do. I warrant it grieves my husband
As if the cause were his.
DESDEMONA
O, that's an honest fellow. Do not doubt, Cassio,
But I will have my lord and you again
As friendly as you were.

58 bosom inmost thoughts

3.2. Location: The citadel.
2 do my duties convey my respects   **3 works** breastworks, fortifications   **4 Repair** return, come   **6 wait upon** attend

3.3. Location: The garden of the citadel.

CASSIO   Bounteous madam,
  Whatever shall become of Michael Cassio,
  He's never anything but your true servant.

DESDEMONA
  I know 't. I thank you. You do love my lord;
  You have known him long, and be you well assured
  He shall in strangeness stand no farther off   12
  Than in a politic distance.

CASSIO   Ay, but, lady,   13
  That policy may either last so long,
  Or feed upon such nice and waterish diet,   15
  Or breed itself so out of circumstance,   16
  That, I being absent and my place supplied,   17
  My general will forget my love and service.

DESDEMONA
  Do not doubt that. Before Emilia here   19
  I give thee warrant of thy place. Assure thee,
  If I do vow a friendship I'll perform it
  To the last article. My lord shall never rest.
  I'll watch him tame and talk him out of patience;   23
  His bed shall seem a school, his board a shrift;   24
  I'll intermingle everything he does
  With Cassio's suit. Therefore be merry, Cassio,
  For thy solicitor shall rather die   27
  Than give thy cause away.   28

      Enter Othello and Iago [at a distance].

EMILIA Madam, here comes my lord.
CASSIO Madam, I'll take my leave.
DESDEMONA Why, stay, and hear me speak.
CASSIO
  Madam, not now. I am very ill at ease,
  Unfit for mine own purposes.
DESDEMONA Well, do your discretion.   *Exit Cassio.* 34

---

12 strangeness aloofness   **13 politic** required by wise policy   **15 Or . . .
diet** or sustain itself at length upon such a trivial and meager means of
support   **16 breed . . . circumstance** continually renew itself so out of
chance events, or yield so few chances for my being pardoned
17 supplied filled by another person   **19 doubt** fear   **23 watch him
tame** tame him by keeping him from sleeping. (A term from falconry.)
out of patience past his endurance   **24 shrift** confessional   **27 solicitor**
advocate   **28 away** up   **34 do your discretion** act according to your own
discretion

IAGO   Ha? I like not that.
OTHELLO   What dost thou say?
IAGO
  Nothing, my lord; or if—I know not what.
OTHELLO
  Was not that Cassio parted from my wife?
IAGO
  Cassio, my lord? No, sure, I cannot think it,
  That he would steal away so guiltylike,
  Seeing you coming.
OTHELLO   I do believe 'twas he.
DESDEMONA   How now, my lord?
  I have been talking with a suitor here,
  A man that languishes in your displeasure.
OTHELLO   Who is 't you mean?
DESDEMONA
  Why, your lieutenant, Cassio. Good my lord,
  If I have any grace or power to move you,
  His present reconciliation take;   49
  For if he be not one that truly loves you,
  That errs in ignorance and not in cunning,   51
  I have no judgment in an honest face.
  I prithee, call him back.
OTHELLO   Went he hence now?
DESDEMONA   Yes, faith, so humbled
  That he hath left part of his grief with me
  To suffer with him. Good love, call him back.
OTHELLO
  Not now, sweet Desdemon. Some other time.
DESDEMONA   But shall 't be shortly?
OTHELLO   The sooner, sweet, for you.
DESDEMONA   Shall 't be tonight at supper?
OTHELLO   No, not tonight.
DESDEMONA   Tomorrow dinner, then?   63
OTHELLO   I shall not dine at home.
  I meet the captains at the citadel.
DESDEMONA
  Why, then, tomorrow night, or Tuesday morn,
  On Tuesday noon, or night, on Wednesday morn.

49 present immediate   **51 in cunning** wittingly   **63 dinner** (The noon-
time meal.)

I prithee, name the time, but let it not
Exceed three days. In faith, he's penitent;
And yet his trespass, in our common reason—   70
Save that, they say, the wars must make example   71
Out of her best—is not almost a fault   72
T' incur a private check. When shall he come?   73
Tell me, Othello. I wonder in my soul
What you would ask me that I should deny,
Or stand so mammering on. What? Michael Cassio,   76
That came a-wooing with you, and so many a time,
When I have spoke of you dispraisingly,
Hath ta'en your part—to have so much to do
To bring him in! By 'r Lady, I could do much—   80

OTHELLO
Prithee, no more. Let him come when he will;
I will deny thee nothing.

DESDEMONA   Why, this is not a boon.
'Tis as I should entreat you wear your gloves,
Or feed on nourishing dishes, or keep you warm,
Or sue to you to do a peculiar profit   86
To your own person. Nay, when I have a suit
Wherein I mean to touch your love indeed,
It shall be full of poise and difficult weight,   89
And fearful to be granted.

OTHELLO   I will deny thee nothing.
Whereon, I do beseech thee, grant me this,   92
To leave me but a little to myself.

DESDEMONA
Shall I deny you? No. Farewell, my lord.

OTHELLO
Farewell, my Desdemona. I'll come to thee straight.   95

DESDEMONA
Emilia, come.—Be as your fancies teach you;   96
Whate'er you be, I am obedient.   *Exit [with Emilia].*

---

70 common reason everyday judgments   **71–72 Save . . . best** were it
not that, as the saying goes, military discipline requires making an
example of the very best men. (*Her* refers to *wars* as a singular con-
cept.)   **72 not almost** scarcely   **73 a private check** even a private repri-
mand   **76 mammering on** wavering about   **80 bring him in** restore him
to favor   **86 peculiar** particular, personal   **89 poise** weight, heaviness;
or equipoise, delicate balance involving hard choice   **92 Whereon** in
return for which   **95 straight** straightway   **96 fancies** inclinations

OTHELLO
  Excellent wretch! Perdition catch my soul   98
  But I do love thee! And when I love thee not,   99
  Chaos is come again.
IAGO My noble lord—
OTHELLO What dost thou say, Iago?
IAGO
  Did Michael Cassio, when you wooed my lady,
  Know of your love?
OTHELLO
  He did, from first to last. Why dost thou ask?
IAGO
  But for a satisfaction of my thought;
  No further harm.
OTHELLO   Why of thy thought, Iago?
IAGO
  I did not think he had been acquainted with her.
OTHELLO
  O, yes, and went between us very oft.
IAGO Indeed?
OTHELLO
  Indeed? Ay, indeed. Discern'st thou aught in that?
  Is he not honest?
IAGO Honest, my lord?
OTHELLO Honest. Ay, honest.
IAGO My lord, for aught I know.
OTHELLO What dost thou think?
IAGO Think, my lord?
OTHELLO
  "Think, my lord?" By heaven, thou echo'st me,
  As if there were some monster in thy thought
  Too hideous to be shown. Thou dost mean something.
  I heard thee say even now, thou lik'st not that,
  When Cassio left my wife. What didst not like?
  And when I told thee he was of my counsel   123
  In my whole course of wooing, thou criedst "Indeed?"
  And didst contract and purse thy brow together   125

98 wretch (A term of affectionate endearment.) **99 But I do** if I do
not **123 of my counsel** in my confidence **125 purse** knit

As if thou then hadst shut up in thy brain
Some horrible conceit. If thou dost love me,   127
Show me thy thought.

IAGO   My lord, you know I love you.

OTHELLO   I think thou dost;
And, for I know thou'rt full of love and honesty,
And weigh'st thy words before thou giv'st them breath,
Therefore these stops of thine fright me the more;   133
For such things in a false disloyal knave
Are tricks of custom, but in a man that's just   135
They're close dilations, working from the heart   136
That passion cannot rule.

IAGO   For Michael Cassio,   137
I dare be sworn I think that he is honest.

OTHELLO
I think so too.

IAGO   Men should be what they seem;
Or those that be not, would they might seem none!   140

OTHELLO
Certain, men should be what they seem.

IAGO
Why, then, I think Cassio's an honest man.

OTHELLO   Nay, yet there's more in this.
I prithee, speak to me as to thy thinkings,
As thou dost ruminate, and give thy worst of thoughts
The worst of words.

IAGO   Good my lord, pardon me.
Though I am bound to every act of duty,
I am not bound to that all slaves are free to.   148
Utter my thoughts? Why, say they are vile and false,
As where's that palace whereinto foul things
Sometimes intrude not? Who has that breast so pure
But some uncleanly apprehensions

---

127 conceit fancy   **133 stops** pauses   **135 of custom** customary
136 close dilations secret or involuntary expressions or delays
137 That passion cannot rule i.e., that are too passionately strong to
be restrained (referring to the workings), or, that cannot rule its own
passions (referring to the heart)   **140 none** i.e., not to be men,
or not seem to be honest   **148 that** that which.   **free to** i.e.,
free with respect to

Keep leets and law days, and in sessions sit   153
With meditations lawful?   154

OTHELLO
Thou dost conspire against thy friend, Iago,   155
If thou but think'st him wronged and mak'st his ear
A stranger to thy thoughts.

IAGO   I do beseech you,
Though I perchance am vicious in my guess—   158
As I confess it is my nature's plague
To spy into abuses, and oft my jealousy   160
Shapes faults that are not—that your wisdom then,   161
From one that so imperfectly conceits,   162
Would take no notice, nor build yourself a trouble
Out of his scattering and unsure observance.   164
It were not for your quiet nor your good,
Nor for my manhood, honesty, and wisdom,
To let you know my thoughts.

OTHELLO   What dost thou mean?

IAGO
Good name in man and woman, dear my lord,
Is the immediate jewel of their souls.   169
Who steals my purse steals trash; 'tis something,
    nothing;
'Twas mine, 'tis his, and has been slave to thousands;
But he that filches from me my good name
Robs me of that which not enriches him
And makes me poor indeed.

OTHELLO   By heaven, I'll know thy thoughts.

IAGO
You cannot, if my heart were in your hand,   176
Nor shall not, whilst 'tis in my custody.

OTHELLO
Ha?

IAGO   O, beware, my lord, of jealousy!

---

153 Keep leets and law days i.e., hold court, set up their authority in
one's heart. (*Leets* are a kind of manor court; *law days* are the days
courts sit in session, or those sessions.)   **154 With** along with.   **lawful**
innocent   **155 thy friend** i.e., Othello   **158 vicious** wrong   **160 jealousy**
suspicion of evil   **161 then** on that account   **162 one** i.e., myself,
Iago.   **conceits** judges, conjectures   **164 scattering** random
169 immediate essential, most precious   **176 if** even if

It is the green-eyed monster which doth mock   179
The meat it feeds on. That cuckold lives in bliss   180
Who, certain of his fate, loves not his wronger;   181
But O, what damnèd minutes tells he o'er   182
Who dotes, yet doubts, suspects, yet fondly loves!
OTHELLO   O misery!
IAGO
Poor and content is rich, and rich enough,   185
But riches fineless is as poor as winter   186
To him that ever fears he shall be poor.
Good God, the souls of all my tribe defend
From jealousy!
OTHELLO   Why, why is this?
Think'st thou I'd make a life of jealousy,
To follow still the changes of the moon   192
With fresh suspicions? No! To be once in doubt   193
Is once to be resolved. Exchange me for a goat   194
When I shall turn the business of my soul
To such exsufflicate and blown surmises   196
Matching thy inference. 'Tis not to make me jealous   197
To say my wife is fair, feeds well, loves company,
Is free of speech, sings, plays, and dances well;
Where virtue is, these are more virtuous.
Nor from mine own weak merits will I draw
The smallest fear or doubt of her revolt,   202
For she had eyes, and chose me. No, Iago,
I'll see before I doubt; when I doubt, prove;
And on the proof, there is no more but this—
Away at once with love or jealousy.

179–180 doth mock . . . on mocks and torments the heart of its victim,
the man who suffers jealousy   181 his wronger i.e., his faithless wife.
(The unsuspecting cuckold is spared the misery of loving his wife only
to discover she is cheating on him.)   182 tells counts   185 Poor . . .
enough to be content with what little one has is the greatest wealth of
all. (Proverbial.)   186 fineless boundless   192–193 To follow . . . suspicions to be constantly imagining new causes for suspicion, changing
incessantly like the moon   194 once once and for all.   resolved free of
doubt, having settled the matter   196 exsufflicate and blown inflated
and blown up, rumored about; or, spat out and flyblown, hence, loath-
some, disgusting   197 inference description or allegation   202 doubt
. . . revolt fear of her unfaithfulness

IAGO

   I am glad of this, for now I shall have reason
   To show the love and duty that I bear you
   With franker spirit. Therefore, as I am bound,
   Receive it from me. I speak not yet of proof.
   Look to your wife; observe her well with Cassio.
   Wear your eyes thus, not jealous nor secure.   212
   I would not have your free and noble nature,
   Out of self-bounty, be abused. Look to 't.   214
   I know our country disposition well;
   In Venice they do let God see the pranks
   They dare not show their husbands; their best
      conscience
   Is not to leave 't undone, but keep 't unknown.

OTHELLO   Dost thou say so?

IAGO

   She did deceive her father, marrying you;
   And when she seemed to shake and fear your looks,
   She loved them most.

OTHELLO   And so she did.

IAGO   Why, go to, then!   222
   She that, so young, could give out such a seeming,   223
   To seel her father's eyes up close as oak,   224
   He thought 'twas witchcraft! But I am much to blame.
   I humbly do beseech you of your pardon
   For too much loving you.

OTHELLO   I am bound to thee forever.   228

IAGO

   I see this hath a little dashed your spirits.

OTHELLO

   Not a jot, not a jot.

IAGO   I' faith, I fear it has.
   I hope you will consider what is spoke
   Comes from my love. But I do see you're moved.
   I am to pray you not to strain my speech

---

212 not neither. **secure** free from uncertainty **214 self-bounty** inher-
ent or natural goodness and generosity. **abused** deceived **222 go to**
(An expression of impatience.) **223 seeming** false appearance **224 seel**
blind. (A term from falconry.) **oak** (A close-grained wood.) **228 bound**
indebted (but perhaps with ironic sense of "tied")

To grosser issues nor to larger reach   234
Than to suspicion.
OTHELLO   I will not.
IAGO   Should you do so, my lord,
My speech should fall into such vile success   238
Which my thoughts aimed not. Cassio's my worthy
   friend.
My lord, I see you're moved.
OTHELLO   No, not much moved.
I do not think but Desdemona's honest.   241
IAGO
Long live she so! And long live you to think so!
OTHELLO
And yet, how nature erring from itself—
IAGO
Ay, there's the point! As—to be bold with you—
Not to affect many proposèd matches   245
Of her own clime, complexion, and degree,
Whereto we see in all things nature tends—
Foh! One may smell in such a will most rank,   248
Foul disproportion, thoughts unnatural.   249
But pardon me. I do not in position   250
Distinctly speak of her, though I may fear
Her will, recoiling to her better judgment,   252
May fall to match you with her country forms   253
And happily repent.
OTHELLO   Farewell, farewell!   254
If more thou dost perceive, let me know more.
Set on thy wife to observe. Leave me, Iago.
IAGO [Going]   My lord, I take my leave.
OTHELLO
Why did I marry? This honest creature doubtless
Sees and knows more, much more, than he unfolds.

---

234 issues significances.   **reach** meaning, scope   **238 success** effect,
result   **241 honest** chaste   **245 affect** prefer, desire   **248 will** sensuality, appetite   **249 disproportion** abnormality   **250 position** argument,
proposition   **252 recoiling** reverting.   **better** i.e., more natural and
reconsidered   **253 fall . . . forms** undertake to compare you with Venetian norms of handsomeness   **254 happily repent** haply repent her
marriage

IAGO [*Returning*]
  My Lord, I would I might entreat your honor
  To scan this thing no farther. Leave it to time.
  Although 'tis fit that Cassio have his place—
  For, sure, he fills it up with great ability—
  Yet, if you please to hold him off awhile,
  You shall by that perceive him and his means.
  Note if your lady strain his entertainment   266
  With any strong or vehement importunity;
  Much will be seen in that. In the meantime,
  Let me be thought too busy in my fears—
  As worthy cause I have to fear I am—
  And hold her free, I do beseech your honor.   271
OTHELLO   Fear not my government.   272
IAGO   I once more take my leave.   *Exit.*
OTHELLO
  This fellow's of exceeding honesty,
  And knows all qualities, with a learnèd spirit,   275
  Of human dealings. If I do prove her haggard,   276
  Though that her jesses were my dear heartstrings,   277
  I'd whistle her off and let her down the wind   278
  To prey at fortune. Haply, for I am black   279
  And have not those soft parts of conversation   280
  That chamberers have, or for I am declined   281
  Into the vale of years—yet that's not much—
  She's gone. I am abused, and my relief   283
  Must be to loathe her. O curse of marriage,
  That we can call these delicate creatures ours
  And not their appetites! I had rather be a toad
  And live upon the vapor of a dungeon
  Than keep a corner in the thing I love
  For others' uses. Yet, 'tis the plague of great ones;
  Prerogatived are they less than the base.   290

---

266 strain his entertainment urge his reinstatement   **271 hold her free**
regard her as innocent   **272 government** self-control, conduct
275 qualities natures, types   **276 haggard** wild (like a wild female
hawk)   **277 jesses** straps fastened around the legs of a trained hawk
278 I'd ... wind i.e., I'd let her go forever. (To release a hawk downwind
was to invite it not to return.)   **279 prey at fortune** fend for herself in
the wild.   **Haply, for** perhaps because   **280 soft ... conversation**
pleasing graces of social behavior   **281 chamberers** gallants
283 abused deceived   **290 Prerogatived** privileged (to have honest
wives).   **the base** ordinary citizens

'Tis destiny unshunnable, like death.
Even then this forkèd plague is fated to us   292
When we do quicken. Look where she comes.   293

    Enter Desdemona and Emilia

If she be false, O, then heaven mocks itself!
I'll not believe 't.
DESDEMONA   How now, my dear Othello?
Your dinner, and the generous islanders   296
By you invited, do attend your presence.   297
OTHELLO
I am to blame.
DESDEMONA   Why do you speak so faintly?
Are you not well?
OTHELLO
I have a pain upon my forehead here.
DESDEMONA
Faith, that's with watching. 'Twill away again.   301
                   [*She offers her handkerchief.*]
Let me but bind it hard, within this hour
It will be well.
OTHELLO   Your napkin is too little.   303
Let it alone. Come, I'll go in with you.   304
           [*He puts the handkerchief from him,
                      and it drops.*]
DESDEMONA
I am very sorry that you are not well.
                      Exit [*with Othello*].
EMILIA [*Picking up the handkerchief*]
I am glad I have found this napkin.
This was her first remembrance from the Moor.
My wayward husband hath a hundred times   308
Wooed me to steal it, but she so loves the token—
For he conjured her she should ever keep it—
That she reserves it evermore about her

---

292 forkèd (An allusion to the horns of the cuckold.) **293 quicken** receive life. (*Quicken* may also mean to swarm with maggots as the body festers, as in 4.2.69, in which case ll. 292–293 suggest that *even then*, in death, we are cuckolded by *forkèd* worms.) **296 generous** noble **297 attend** await **301 watching** too little sleep **303 napkin** handkerchief **304 Let it alone** i.e., never mind **308 wayward** capricious

To kiss and talk to. I'll have the work ta'en out,   312
And give 't Iago. What he will do with it
Heaven knows, not I;
I nothing but to please his fantasy.   315

    Enter Iago.

IAGO
How now? What do you here alone?
EMILIA
Do not you chide. I have a thing for you.
IAGO
You have a thing for me? It is a common thing—   318
EMILIA Ha?
IAGO To have a foolish wife.
EMILIA
O, is that all? What will you give me now
For that same handkerchief?
IAGO What handkerchief?
EMILIA What handkerchief?
Why, that the Moor first gave to Desdemona;
That which so often you did bid me steal.
IAGO Hast stolen it from her?
EMILIA
No, faith. She let it drop by negligence,
And to th' advantage I, being here, took 't up.   329
Look, here 'tis.
IAGO   A good wench! Give it me.
EMILIA
What will you do with 't, that you have been so earnest
To have me filch it?
IAGO [*Snatching it*]   Why, what is that to you?
EMILIA
If it be not for some purpose of import,
Give 't me again. Poor lady, she'll run mad
When she shall lack it.
IAGO   Be not acknown on 't.   335
I have use for it. Go, leave me.   *Exit Emilia.*

---

312 work ta'en out design of the embroidery copied   **315 fantasy**
whim   **318 common thing** (with bawdy suggestion; *common* suggests
coarseness and availability to all comers, and *thing* is a slang term for
the pudendum)   **329 to th' advantage** taking the opportunity   **335 Be
. . . on 't** do not confess knowledge of it

I will in Cassio's lodging lose this napkin   337
And let him find it. Trifles light as air
Are to the jealous confirmations strong
As proofs of Holy Writ. This may do something.
The Moor already changes with my poison.
Dangerous conceits are in their natures poisons,   342
Which at the first are scarce found to distaste,   343
But with a little act upon the blood   344
Burn like the mines of sulfur.

    Enter Othello.

                          I did say so.
Look where he comes! Not poppy nor mandragora   346
Nor all the drowsy syrups of the world
Shall ever medicine thee to that sweet sleep
Which thou owedst yesterday.

OTHELLO   Ha, ha, false to me?   349

IAGO
Why, how now, General? No more of that.

OTHELLO
Avaunt! Begone! Thou hast set me on the rack.
I swear 'tis better to be much abused
Than but to know 't a little.

IAGO   How now, my lord?

OTHELLO
What sense had I of her stolen hours of lust?
I saw 't not, thought it not, it harmed not me.
I slept the next night well, fed well, was free and merry;   356
I found not Cassio's kisses on her lips.
He that is robbed, not wanting what is stolen,   358
Let him not know 't and he's not robbed at all.

IAGO   I am sorry to hear this.

OTHELLO
I had been happy if the general camp,
Pioners and all, had tasted her sweet body,   362
So I had nothing known. O, now, forever   363

---

337 lose (The Folio spelling, *loose,* is a normal spelling for "lose," but it may also contain the idea of "let go," "release.") **342 conceits** fancies, ideas **343 distaste** be distasteful **344 act** action, working **346 mandragora** an opiate made of the mandrake root **349 thou owedst** you did own **356 free** carefree **358 wanting** missing **362 Pioneers** diggers of mines, the lowest grade of soldiers **363 So** provided

Farewell the tranquil mind! Farewell content!
Farewell the plumèd troops and the big wars   365
That makes ambition virtue! O, farewell!
Farewell the neighing steed and the shrill trump,
The spirit-stirring drum, th' ear-piercing fife,
The royal banner, and all quality,   369
Pride, pomp, and circumstance of glorious war!   370
And O, you mortal engines, whose rude throats   371
Th' immortal Jove's dread clamors counterfeit,   372
Farewell! Othello's occupation's gone.

IAGO Is 't possible, my lord?

OTHELLO
Villain, be sure thou prove my love a whore!
Be sure of it. Give me the ocular proof,
Or, by the worth of mine eternal soul,
Thou hadst been better have been born a dog
Than answer my waked wrath!

IAGO   Is 't come to this?

OTHELLO
Make me to see 't, or at the least so prove it
That the probation bear no hinge nor loop   381
To hang a doubt on, or woe upon thy life!

IAGO My noble lord—

OTHELLO
If thou dost slander her and torture me,
Never pray more; abandon all remorse;   385
On horror's head horrors accumulate;   386
Do deeds to make heaven weep, all earth amazed;   387
For nothing canst thou to damnation add
Greater than that.

IAGO   O grace! O heaven forgive me!
Are you a man? Have you a soul or sense?
God b' wi' you; take mine office. O wretched fool,   391
That lov'st to make thine honesty a vice!   392
O monstrous world! Take note, take note, O world,

---

365 **big** stately   369 **quality** character, essential nature   370 **Pride** rich
display.   **circumstance** pageantry   371 **mortal engines** i.e., cannon.
(*Mortal* means "deadly.")   372 **Jove's dread clamors** i.e., thunder
381 **probation** proof   385 **remorse** pity   386 **horrors accumulate** add
still more horrors   387 **amazed** confounded with horror   391 **O
wretched fool** (Iago addresses himself as a fool for having carried
honesty too far.)   392 **vice** failing, something overdone

To be direct and honest is not safe.
I thank you for this profit, and from hence   395
I'll love no friend, sith love breeds such offense. 396
OTHELLO   Nay, stay. Thou shouldst be honest.   397
IAGO
  I should be wise, for honesty's a fool
  And loses that it works for.
OTHELLO   By the world,   399
  I think my wife be honest and think she is not;
  I think that thou art just and think thou art not.
  I'll have some proof. My name, that was as fresh
  As Dian's visage, is now begrimed and black   403
  As mine own face. If there be cords, or knives,
  Poison, or fire, or suffocating streams,
  I'll not endure it. Would I were satisfied!
IAGO
  I see, sir, you are eaten up with passion.
  I do repent me that I put it to you.
  You would be satisfied?
OTHELLO   Would? Nay, and I will.
IAGO
  And may; but how? How satisfied, my lord?
  Would you, the supervisor, grossly gape on?   411
  Behold her topped?
OTHELLO   Death and damnation! O!
IAGO
  It were a tedious difficulty, I think,
  To bring them to that prospect. Damn them then,   414
  If ever mortal eyes do see them bolster   415
  More than their own. What then? How then?   416
  What shall I say? Where's satisfaction?
  It is impossible you should see this,
  Were they as prime as goats, as hot as monkeys,   419
  As salt as wolves in pride, and fools as gross   420

---

395 **profit** profitable instruction. **hence** henceforth 396 **sith** since.
offense i.e., harm to the one who offers help and friendship 397 **Thou**
shouldst be it appears that you are. (But Iago replies in the sense of
"ought to be.") 399 **that** what 403 **Dian** Diana, goddess of the moon
and of chastity 411 **supervisor** onlooker 414 **Damn them then** i.e.,
they would have to be really incorrigible 415 **bolster** go to bed together, share a bolster 416 **More** other 419 **prime** lustful 420 **salt**
wanton, sensual. **pride** heat

As ignorance made drunk. But yet, I say,
If imputation and strong circumstances
Which lead directly to the door of truth
Will give you satisfaction, you might have 't.

OTHELLO
Give me a living reason she's disloyal.

IAGO   I do not like the office.
But sith I am entered in this cause so far,   427
Pricked to 't by foolish honesty and love,   428
I will go on. I lay with Cassio lately,
And being troubled with a raging tooth
I could not sleep. There are a kind of men
So loose of soul that in their sleeps will mutter
Their affairs. One of this kind is Cassio.
In sleep I heard him say, "Sweet Desdemona,
Let us be wary, let us hide our loves!"
And then, sir, would he grip and wring my hand,
Cry "O sweet creature!" then kiss me hard,
As if he plucked up kisses by the roots
That grew upon my lips; then laid his leg
Over my thigh, and sighed, and kissed, and then
Cried, "Cursèd fate that gave thee to the Moor!"

OTHELLO
O monstrous! Monstrous!

IAGO   Nay, this was but his dream.

OTHELLO
But this denoted a foregone conclusion.   443
'Tis a shrewd doubt, though it be but a dream.   444

IAGO
And this may help to thicken other proofs
That do demonstrate thinly.

OTHELLO   I'll tear her all to pieces.

IAGO
Nay, yet be wise. Yet we see nothing done;
She may be honest yet. Tell me but this:
Have you not sometimes seen a handkerchief
Spotted with strawberries in your wife's hand?   450

427 sith since   **428 Pricked** spurred   **443 foregone conclusion** concluded experience or action   **444 shrewd doubt** suspicious circumstance   **450 Spotted with strawberries** embroidered with a strawberry pattern

OTHELLO
  I gave her such a one. 'Twas my first gift.
IAGO
  I know not that; but such a handkerchief—
  I am sure it was your wife's—did I today
  See Cassio wipe his beard with.
OTHELLO   If it be that—
IAGO
  If it be that, or any that was hers,
  It speaks against her with the other proofs.
OTHELLO
  O, that the slave had forty thousand lives!   457
  One is too poor, too weak for my revenge.
  Now do I see 'tis true. Look here, Iago,
  All my fond love thus do I blow to heaven.   460
  'Tis gone.
  Arise, black vengeance, from the hollow hell!
  Yield up, O love, thy crown and hearted throne   463
  To tyrannous hate! Swell, bosom, with thy freight,   464
  For 'tis of aspics' tongues!   465
IAGO   Yet be content.   466
OTHELLO   O, blood, blood, blood!
IAGO
  Patience, I say. Your mind perhaps may change.
OTHELLO
  Never, Iago. Like to the Pontic Sea,   469
  Whose icy current and compulsive course
  Ne'er feels retiring ebb, but keeps due on
  To the Propontic and the Hellespont,   472
  Even so my bloody thoughts with violent pace
  Shall ne'er look back, ne'er ebb to humble love,
  Till that a capable and wide revenge   475
  Swallow them up. Now, by yond marble heaven,   476
  [Kneeling] In the due reverence of a sacred vow
  I here engage my words.

457 the slave i.e., Cassio   460 fond foolish   463 hearted fixed in
the heart   464 freight burden   465 aspics' venomous serpents'
466 content calm   469 Pontic Sea Black Sea   472 Propontic body of
water between the Bosporus and Hellespont   475 capable comprehen-
sive   476 marble i.e., gleaming like marble

IAGO   Do not rise yet.
[*He kneels.*] Witness, you ever-burning lights above,   479
You elements that clip us round about,   480
Witness that here Iago doth give up
The execution of his wit, hands, heart,   482
To wronged Othello's service! Let him command,
And to obey shall be in me remorse,   484
What bloody business ever.   [*They rise.*]
OTHELLO   I greet thy love,   485
Not with vain thanks, but with acceptance bounteous,
And will upon the instant put thee to 't.
Within these three days let me hear thee say
That Cassio's not alive.
IAGO   My friend is dead;
'Tis done at your request. But let her live.
OTHELLO
Damn her, lewd minx! O, damn her, damn her!   491
Come, go with me apart. I will withdraw
To furnish me with some swift means of death
For the fair devil. Now art thou my lieutenant.
IAGO   I am your own forever.   *Exeunt.*

❖

3.4   *Enter Desdemona, Emilia, and Clown.*

DESDEMONA Do you know, sirrah, where Lieutenant   1
   Cassio lies?   2
CLOWN   I dare not say he lies anywhere.
DESDEMONA Why, man?
CLOWN   He's a soldier, and for me to say a soldier lies,
   'tis stabbing.
DESDEMONA Go to. Where lodges he?
CLOWN   To tell you where he lodges is to tell you where
   I lie.

479 s.d. He kneels (In the quarto text, Iago kneels here after Othello has
knelt at l. 477.) **480 clip** encompass **482 execution** exercise, action.
wit mind **484 remorse** pity (for Othello's wrongs) **485 ever** soever
491 minx wanton

3.4. Location: Before the citadel.
1 sirrah (A form of address to an inferior.) **2 lies** lodges. (But the Clown
makes the obvious pun.)

DESDEMONA   Can anything be made of this?

CLOWN   I know not where he lodges, and for me to devise a lodging and say he lies here, or he lies there, were to lie in mine own throat.   13

DESDEMONA   Can you inquire him out, and be edified by report?

CLOWN   I will catechize the world for him; that is, make questions, and by them answer.

DESDEMONA   Seek him, bid him come hither. Tell him I have moved my lord on his behalf and hope all will be   19 well.

CLOWN   To do this is within the compass of man's wit, and therefore I will attempt the doing it.   *Exit Clown.*

DESDEMONA
Where should I lose that handkerchief, Emilia?

EMILIA   I know not, madam.

DESDEMONA
Believe me, I had rather have lost my purse
Full of crusadoes; and but my noble Moor   26
Is true of mind and made of no such baseness
As jealous creatures are, it were enough
To put him to ill thinking.

EMILIA   Is he not jealous?

DESDEMONA
Who, he? I think the sun where he was born
Drew all such humors from him.

EMILIA   Look where he comes.   31

        Enter Othello.

DESDEMONA
I will not leave him now till Cassio
Be called to him.—How is 't with you, my lord?

OTHELLO
Well, my good lady. [*Aside.*] O, hardness to dissemble!—
How do you, Desdemona?

DESDEMONA   Well, my good lord.

OTHELLO
Give me your hand. [*She gives her hand.*] This hand is
moist, my lady.

---

13 lie . . . throat lie egregiously and deliberately   **19 moved** petitioned
26 crusadoes Portuguese gold coins   **31 humors** (Refers to the four
bodily fluids thought to determine temperament.)

DESDEMONA
    It yet hath felt no age nor known no sorrow.
OTHELLO
    This argues fruitfulness and liberal heart.   38
    Hot, hot, and moist. This hand of yours requires
    A sequester from liberty, fasting and prayer,   40
    Much castigation, exercise devout;   41
    For here's a young and sweating devil here
    That commonly rebels. 'Tis a good hand,
    A frank one.
DESDEMONA   You may indeed say so,   44
    For 'twas that hand that gave away my heart.
OTHELLO
    A liberal hand! The hearts of old gave hands,   46
    But our new heraldry is hands, not hearts.   47
DESDEMONA
    I cannot speak of this. Come now, your promise.
OTHELLO   What promise, chuck?   49
DESDEMONA
    I have sent to bid Cassio come speak with you.
OTHELLO
    I have a salt and sorry rheum offends me;   51
    Lend me thy handkerchief.
DESDEMONA   Here, my lord. [*She offers a handkerchief.*]
OTHELLO
    That which I gave you.
DESDEMONA   I have it not about me.
OTHELLO   Not?
DESDEMONA   No, faith, my lord.
OTHELLO   That's a fault. That handkerchief
    Did an Egyptian to my mother give.
    She was a charmer, and could almost read   59
    The thoughts of people. She told her, while she kept it,

38 argues gives evidence of. **fruitfulness** generosity, amorousness, and
fecundity. **liberal** generous and sexually free **40 sequester** separation,
sequestration **41 castigation** corrective discipline **44 frank** generous,
open (with sexual suggestion) **46 The hearts . . . hands** i.e., in former
times people would give their hearts when they gave their hands to
something **47 But . . . hearts** i.e., in our decadent times the joining of
hands is no longer a badge to signify the giving of hearts **49 chuck** (A
term of endearment.) **51 salt . . . rheum** distressful head cold or water-
ing of the eyes **59 charmer** sorceress

'Twould make her amiable and subdue my father   61
Entirely to her love, but if she lost it
Or made a gift of it, my father's eye
Should hold her loathèd and his spirits should hunt
After new fancies. She, dying, gave it me,   65
And bid me, when my fate would have me wived,
To give it her. I did so; and take heed on 't;   67
Make it a darling like your precious eye.
To lose 't or give 't away were such perdition   69
As nothing else could match.

DESDEMONA   Is 't possible?

OTHELLO
'Tis true. There's magic in the web of it.   71
A sibyl, that had numbered in the world
The sun to course two hundred compasses,   73
In her prophetic fury sewed the work;   74
The worms were hallowed that did breed the silk,
And it was dyed in mummy which the skillful   76
Conserved of maidens' hearts.

DESDEMONA   I' faith! Is 't true?   77

OTHELLO
Most veritable. Therefore look to 't well.

DESDEMONA
Then would to God that I had never seen 't!

OTHELLO   Ha? Wherefore?

DESDEMONA
Why do you speak so startingly and rash?   81

OTHELLO
Is 't lost? Is 't gone? Speak, is 't out o' the way?   82

DESDEMONA   Heaven bless us!

OTHELLO   Say you?

DESDEMONA
It is not lost; but what an if it were?   85

OTHELLO   How?

---

61 amiable desirable   **65 fancies** loves   **67 her** i.e., to my wife
69 perdition loss   **71 web** fabric, weaving   **73 compasses** annual cir-
clings. (The *sibyl*, or prophetess, was 200 years old.)   **74 prophetic fury**
frenzy of prophetic inspiration   **76 mummy** medicinal or magical
preparation drained from mummified bodies   **77 Conserved of** prepared or preserved out of   **81 startingly and rash** disjointedly and
impetuously, excitedly   **82 out o' the way** lost, misplaced   **85 an if** if

DESDEMONA
  I say it is not lost.
OTHELLO   Fetch 't. Let me see 't.
DESDEMONA
  Why, so I can, sir, but I will not now.
  This is a trick to put me from my suit.
  Pray you, let Cassio be received again.
OTHELLO
  Fetch me the handkerchief! My mind misgives.
DESDEMONA Come, come,
  You'll never meet a more sufficient man.   93
OTHELLO
  The handkerchief!
DESDEMONA   I pray, talk me of Cassio.   94
OTHELLO
  The handkerchief!
DESDEMONA   A man that all his time   95
  Hath founded his good fortunes on your love,
  Shared dangers with you—
OTHELLO The handkerchief!
DESDEMONA I' faith, you are to blame.
OTHELLO Zounds!   *Exit Othello.*
EMILIA Is not this man jealous?
DESDEMONA I ne'er saw this before.
  Sure, there's some wonder in this handkerchief.
  I am most unhappy in the loss of it.
EMILIA
  'Tis not a year or two shows us a man.   105
  They are all but stomachs, and we all but food;   106
  They eat us hungerly, and when they are full   107
  They belch us.

        Enter Iago and Cassio.

                    Look you, Cassio and my husband.
IAGO
  There is no other way; 'tis she must do 't.
  And, lo, the happiness! Go and importune her.   110

93 sufficient able, complete   **94 talk** talk to   **95 all his time** throughout
his career   **105 'Tis . . . man** i.e., you can't really know a man even
in a year or two of experience (?) or, real men come along seldom (?)
106 but nothing but   **107 hungerly** hungrily   **110 the happiness** in
happy time, fortunately met

DESDEMONA
    How now, good Cassio? What's the news with you?
CASSIO
    Madam, my former suit. I do beseech you
    That by your virtuous means I may again   113
    Exist, and be a member of his love
    Whom I with all the office of my heart   115
    Entirely honor. I would not be delayed.
    If my offense be of such mortal kind   117
    That nor my service past nor present sorrows,   118
    Nor purposed merit in futurity,
    Can ransom me into his love again,
    But to know so must be my benefit;   121
    So shall I clothe me in a forced content,
    And shut myself up in some other course,
    To fortune's alms.
DESDEMONA   Alas, thrice-gentle Cassio,   124
    My advocation is not now in tune.   125
    My lord is not my lord; nor should I know him,
    Were he in favor as in humor altered.   127
    So help me every spirit sanctified
    As I have spoken for you all my best
    And stood within the blank of his displeasure   130
    For my free speech! You must awhile be patient.
    What I can do I will, and more I will
    Than for myself I dare. Let that suffice you.
IAGO
    Is my lord angry?
EMILIA   He went hence but now,
    And certainly in strange unquietness.
IAGO
    Can he be angry? I have seen the cannon
    When it hath blown his ranks into the air,
    And like the devil from his very arm
    Puffed his own brother—and is he angry?

113 **virtuous** efficacious   115 **office** loyal service   117 **mortal** fatal
118 **nor . . . nor** neither . . . nor   121 **But . . . benefit** merely to know
that my case is hopeless must be all I can expect   124 **To fortune's
alms** throwing myself on the mercy of fortune   125 **advocation** advocacy   127 **favor** appearance   130 **within the blank** within point-blank
range. (The *blank* is the center of the target.)

Something of moment then. I will go meet him.   140
There's matter in 't indeed, if he be angry.

DESDEMONA
    I prithee, do so.   *Exit [Iago].*
                        Something, sure, of state,   142
Either from Venice, or some unhatched practice   143
Made demonstrable here in Cyprus to him,
Hath puddled his clear spirit; and in such cases   145
Men's natures wrangle with inferior things,
Though great ones are their object. 'Tis even so;
For let our finger ache, and it indues   148
Our other healthful members even to a sense
Of pain. Nay, we must think men are not gods,
Nor of them look for such observancy   151
As fits the bridal. Beshrew me much, Emilia,   152
I was, unhandsome warrior as I am,   153
Arraigning his unkindness with my soul;   154
But now I find I had suborned the witness,   155
And he's indicted falsely.

EMILIA   Pray heaven it be
State matters, as you think, and no conception
Nor no jealous toy concerning you.   158

DESDEMONA
    Alas the day! I never gave him cause.

EMILIA
    But jealous souls will not be answered so;
    They are not ever jealous for the cause,
    But jealous for they're jealous. It is a monster   162
    Begot upon itself, born on itself.   163

DESDEMONA
    Heaven keep that monster from Othello's mind!

EMILIA   Lady, amen.

DESDEMONA
    I will go seek him. Cassio, walk hereabout.

140 of moment of immediate importance, momentous   **142 of state**
concerning state affairs   **143 unhatched practice** as yet unexecuted or
undiscovered plot   **145 puddled** muddied   **148 indues** brings to the
same condition   **151 observancy** attentiveness   **152 bridal** wedding
(when a bridegroom is newly attentive to his bride).   **Beshrew me** (A
mild oath.)   **153 unhandsome** insufficient, unskillful   **154 with** before
the bar of   **155 suborned the witness** induced the witness to give false
testimony   **158 toy** fancy   **162 for** because   **163 Begot upon itself**
generated solely from itself

If I do find him fit, I'll move your suit
And seek to effect it to my uttermost.
CASSIO   I humbly thank your ladyship.
                          Exit [*Desdemona with Emilia*].

        Enter Bianca.

BIANCA
  Save you, friend Cassio!
CASSIO   What make you from home?   170
  How is 't with you, my most fair Bianca?
  I' faith, sweet love, I was coming to your house.
BIANCA
  And I was going to your lodging, Cassio.
  What, keep a week away? Seven days and nights?
  Eightscore-eight hours? And lovers' absent hours
  More tedious than the dial eightscore times?   176
  O weary reckoning!
CASSIO   Pardon me, Bianca.
  I have this while with leaden thoughts been pressed;
  But I shall, in a more continuate time,   179
  Strike off this score of absence. Sweet Bianca, 180
          [*Giving her Desdemona's handkerchief*]
  Take me this work out.
BIANCA   O Cassio, whence came this?   181
  This is some token from a newer friend.   182
  To the felt absence now I feel a cause.
  Is 't come to this? Well, well.
CASSIO   Go to, woman!
  Throw your vile guesses in the devil's teeth,
  From whence you have them. You are jealous now
  That this is from some mistress, some remembrance.
  No, by my faith, Bianca.
BIANCA   Why, whose is it?
CASSIO
  I know not, neither. I found it in my chamber.
  I like the work well. Ere it be demanded—   190
  As like enough it will—I would have it copied.   191
  Take it and do 't, and leave me for this time.

---

170 **Save** God save.   **make** do   176 **the dial** a complete revolution of the
clock   179 **continuate** uninterrupted   180 **Strike . . . score** settle this
account   181 **Take . . . out** copy this embroidery for me   182 **friend**
mistress   190 **demanded** inquired for   191 **like** likely

BIANCA   Leave you? Wherefore?

CASSIO
  I do attend here on the General,
  And think it no addition, nor my wish,   195
  To have him see me womaned.

BIANCA   Why, I pray you?

CASSIO   Not that I love you not.

BIANCA   But that you do not love me.
  I pray you, bring me on the way a little,   200
  And say if I shall see you soon at night.

CASSIO
  'Tis but a little way that I can bring you,
  For I attend here; but I'll see you soon.

BIANCA
  'Tis very good. I must be circumstanced.   204

                    Exeunt omnes.

                    ❖

---

195 addition i.e., addition to my reputation   **200 bring** accompany
204 be circumstanced be governed by circumstance, yield to your
conditions

4.1 *Enter Othello and Iago.*

IAGO
Will you think so?

OTHELLO   Think so, Iago?

IAGO   What,
To kiss in private?

OTHELLO   An unauthorized kiss!

IAGO
Or to be naked with her friend in bed
An hour or more, not meaning any harm?

OTHELLO
Naked in bed, Iago, and not mean harm?
It is hypocrisy against the devil.
They that mean virtuously, and yet do so,
The devil their virtue tempts, and they tempt heaven.

IAGO
If they do nothing, 'tis a venial slip.   9
But if I give my wife a handkerchief—

OTHELLO   What then?

IAGO
Why then, 'tis hers, my lord, and being hers,
She may, I think, bestow 't on any man.

OTHELLO
She is protectress of her honor too.
May she give that?

IAGO
Her honor is an essence that's not seen;
They have it very oft that have it not.   17
But, for the handkerchief—

OTHELLO
By heaven, I would most gladly have forgot it.
Thou saidst—O, it comes o'er my memory
As doth the raven o'er the infectious house,   21
Boding to all—he had my handkerchief.

IAGO
Ay, what of that?

4.1. Location: Before the citadel.
9 venial pardonable   **17 They have it** i.e., they enjoy a reputation for
it   **21 raven . . . house** (Allusion to the belief that the raven hovered over
a house of sickness or infection, such as one visited by the plague.)

OTHELLO   That's not so good now.
IAGO   What
  If I had said I had seen him do you wrong?
  Or heard him say—as knaves be such abroad,   25
  Who having, by their own importunate suit,
  Or voluntary dotage of some mistress,   27
  Convincèd or supplied them, cannot choose   28
  But they must blab—
OTHELLO   Hath he said anything?
IAGO
  He hath, my lord; but, be you well assured,
  No more than he'll unswear.
OTHELLO   What hath he said?
IAGO
  Faith, that he did—I know not what he did.
OTHELLO   What? What?
IAGO
  Lie—
OTHELLO   With her?
IAGO   With her, on her; what you will.
OTHELLO   Lie with her? Lie on her? We say "lie on her"
  when they belie her. Lie with her? Zounds, that's ful- 36
  some.—Handkerchief—confessions—handkerchief!   37
  —To confess and be hanged for his labor—first to be   38
  hanged and then to confess.—I tremble at it. Nature   39
  would not invest herself in such shadowing passion   40
  without some instruction. It is not words that shakes   41
  me thus. Pish! Noses, ears, and lips.—Is 't possible?—
  Confess—handkerchief!—O devil!
                                        Falls in a trance.

IAGO   Work on,
  My medicine, work! Thus credulous fools are caught,
  And many worthy and chaste dames even thus,

---

25 abroad around about   **27 voluntary dotage** willing infatuation
28 Convincèd or supplied seduced or gratified   **36 belie** slander
36–37 fulsome foul   **38–39 first . . . to confess** (Othello reverses the
proverbial *confess and be hanged;* Cassio is to be given no time to
confess before he dies.)   **39–41 Nature . . . instruction** i.e., without some
foundation in fact, nature would not have dressed herself in such an
overwhelming passion that comes over me now and fills my mind with
images, or in such a lifelike fantasy as Cassio had in his dream of lying
with Desdemona   **41 words** mere words

All guiltless, meet reproach.—What ho! My lord!
My lord, I say! Othello!

    Enter Cassio.

             How now, Cassio?

CASSIO What's the matter?

IAGO
My lord is fall'n into an epilepsy.
This is his second fit. He had one yesterday.

CASSIO
Rub him about the temples.

IAGO   No, forbear.
The lethargy must have his quiet course.   53
If not, he foams at mouth, and by and by
Breaks out to savage madness. Look, he stirs.
Do you withdraw yourself a little while.
He will recover straight. When he is gone,
I would on great occasion speak with you.   58
                       [Exit Cassio.]
How is it, General? Have you not hurt your head?

OTHELLO
Dost thou mock me?

IAGO   I mock you not, by heaven.   60
Would you would bear your fortune like a man!

OTHELLO
A hornèd man's a monster and a beast.

IAGO
There's many a beast then in a populous city,
And many a civil monster.   64

OTHELLO Did he confess it?

IAGO Good sir, be a man.
Think every bearded fellow that's but yoked   67
May draw with you. There's millions now alive   68
That nightly lie in those unproper beds   69

---

53 lethargy coma. **his** its **58 on great occasion** on a matter of great importance **60 mock** (Othello takes Iago's question about hurting his head to be a mocking reference to the cuckold's horns.) **64 civil** i.e., dwelling in a city **67 yoked** (1) married (2) put into the yoke of infamy and cuckoldry **68 draw with you** pull as you do like oxen who are yoked, i.e., share your fate as cuckold **69 unproper** not exclusively their own

Which they dare swear peculiar. Your case is better.   70
O, 'tis the spite of hell, the fiend's arch-mock,
To lip a wanton in a secure couch   72
And to suppose her chaste! No, let me know,
And knowing what I am, I know what she shall be.   74
OTHELLO   O, thou art wise. 'Tis certain.
IAGO   Stand you awhile apart;
  Confine yourself but in a patient list.   77
  Whilst you were here o'erwhelmèd with your grief—
  A passion most unsuiting such a man—
  Cassio came hither. I shifted him away,   80
  And laid good 'scuses upon your ecstasy,   81
  Bade him anon return and here speak with me,
  The which he promised. Do but encave yourself   83
  And mark the fleers, the gibes, and notable scorns   84
  That dwell in every region of his face;
  For I will make him tell the tale anew,
  Where, how, how oft, how long ago, and when
  He hath and is again to cope your wife.   88
  I say, but mark his gesture. Marry, patience!
  Or I shall say you're all-in-all in spleen,   90
  And nothing of a man.
OTHELLO   Dost thou hear, Iago?
  I will be found most cunning in my patience;
  But—dost thou hear?—most bloody.
IAGO   That's not amiss;
  But yet keep time in all. Will you withdraw?   94
                    [Othello stands apart.]
  Now will I question Cassio of Bianca,
  A huswife that by selling her desires   96
  Buys herself bread and clothes. It is a creature
  That dotes on Cassio—as 'tis the strumpet's plague
  To beguile many and be beguiled by one.

---

70 peculiar private, their own.   **better** i.e., because you know the
truth   **72 lip** kiss.   **secure** free from suspicion   **74 what I am** i.e., a
çuckold.   **she shall be** i.e., an adulteress who must die   **77 in . . . list**
within the bounds of patience   **80 shifted him away** used a dodge to get
rid of him   **81 ecstasy** trance   **83 encave** conceal   **84 fleers** sneers.
notable obvious   **88 cope** encounter with, have sex with   **90 all-in-all in
spleen** utterly governed by passionate impulses   **94 keep time** keep
yourself steady (as in music)   **96 huswife** hussy

He, when he hears of her, cannot restrain   100
From the excess of laughter. Here he comes.

    Enter Cassio.

As he shall smile, Othello shall go mad;
And his unbookish jealousy must conster   103
Poor Cassio's smiles, gestures, and light behaviors
Quite in the wrong.—How do you now, Lieutenant?

CASSIO
The worser that you give me the addition   106
Whose want even kills me.

IAGO
Ply Desdemona well and you are sure on 't.
[*Speaking lower.*] Now, if this suit lay in Bianca's power,
How quickly should you speed!

CASSIO [*Laughing*]   Alas, poor caitiff!   111

OTHELLO   Look how he laughs already!

IAGO
I never knew a woman love man so.

CASSIO
Alas, poor rogue! I think, i' faith, she loves me.

OTHELLO
Now he denies it faintly, and laughs it out.

IAGO
Do you hear, Cassio?

OTHELLO   Now he importunes him
To tell it o'er. Go to! Well said, well said.   117

IAGO
She gives it out that you shall marry her.
Do you intend it?

CASSIO   Ha, ha, ha!

OTHELLO
Do you triumph, Roman? Do you triumph?   121

CASSIO   I marry her? What? A customer? Prithee, bear 122
some charity to my wit; do not think it so unwhole- 123
some. Ha, ha, ha!

---

100 restrain refrain   **103 unbookish** uninstructed. **conster** construe
106 addition title   **111 caitiff** wretch **117 Well said** well done
121 Roman (The Romans were noted for their *triumphs* or triumphal
processions.) **122 customer** i.e., prostitute **122–123 bear . . . wit** be
more charitable to my judgment

OTHELLO So, so, so, so! They laugh that win.   125
IAGO Faith, the cry goes that you shall marry her.   126
CASSIO Prithee, say true.
IAGO I am a very villain else.
OTHELLO Have you scored me? Well.   129
CASSIO This is the monkey's own giving out. She is
   persuaded I will marry her, out of her own love and
   flattery, not out of my promise.   132
OTHELLO Iago beckons me. Now he begins the story.   133
CASSIO She was here even now; she haunts me in every
   place. I was the other day talking on the seabank with
   certain Venetians, and thither comes the bauble, and,   136
   by this hand, she falls me thus about my neck—
                              [He embraces Iago.]
OTHELLO Crying, "O dear Cassio!" as it were; his ges-
   ture imports it.
CASSIO So hangs and lolls and weeps upon me, so
   shakes and pulls me. Ha, ha, ha!
OTHELLO Now he tells how she plucked him to my
   chamber. O, I see that nose of yours, but not that dog
   I shall throw it to.
CASSIO Well, I must leave her company.
IAGO Before me, look where she comes.   146

        Enter Bianca [with Othello's handkerchief].

CASSIO 'Tis such another fitchew! Marry, a perfumed   147
   one.—What do you mean by this haunting of me?
BIANCA Let the devil and his dam haunt you! What did   149
   you mean by that same handkerchief you gave me
   even now? I was a fine fool to take it. I must take out
   the work? A likely piece of work, that you should find   152
   it in your chamber and know not who left it there!
   This is some minx's token, and I must take out the

---

125 They . . . win i.e., they that laugh last laugh best   **126 cry** rumor
129 scored me scored off me, beaten me, made up my reckoning,
branded me   **132 flattery** self-flattery, self-deception   **133 beckons**
signals   **136 bauble** plaything   **146 Before me** i.e., on my soul   **147 'Tis
. . . fitchew** what a polecat she is! Just like all the others.   **fitchew**
(Polecats were often compared with prostitutes because of their rank
smell and presumed lechery.)   **149 dam** mother   **152 A likely . . . work**
a fine story

work? There; give it your hobbyhorse. [*She gives him*   155
the handkerchief.] Wheresoever you had it, I'll take out
no work on 't.

CASSIO   How now, my sweet Bianca? How now? How now?

OTHELLO   By heaven, that should be my handkerchief!   159

BIANCA   If you'll come to supper tonight, you may; if
you will not, come when you are next prepared for.   161
                             Exit.

IAGO   After her, after her.

CASSIO   Faith, I must. She'll rail in the streets else.

IAGO   Will you sup there?

CASSIO   Faith, I intend so.

IAGO   Well, I may chance to see you, for I would very
fain speak with you.

CASSIO   Prithee, come. Will you?

IAGO   Go to. Say no more.   [*Exit Cassio.*]   169

OTHELLO [*Advancing*]   How shall I murder him, Iago?

IAGO   Did you perceive how he laughed at his vice?

OTHELLO   O, Iago!

IAGO   And did you see the handkerchief?

OTHELLO   Was that mine?

IAGO   Yours, by this hand. And to see how he prizes
the foolish woman your wife! She gave it him, and he
hath given it his whore.

OTHELLO   I would have him nine years a-killing. A fine
woman! A fair woman! A sweet woman!

IAGO   Nay, you must forget that.

OTHELLO   Ay, let her rot, and perish, and be damned
tonight, for she shall not live. No, my heart is turned
to stone; I strike it, and it hurts my hand. O, the world
hath not a sweeter creature! She might lie by an em-
peror's side and command him tasks.

IAGO   Nay, that's not your way.   186

OTHELLO   Hang her! I do but say what she is. So delicate
with her needle! An admirable musician! O, she will
sing the savageness out of a bear. Of so high and plen-
teous wit and invention!   190

---

155 hobbyhorse harlot   **159 should be** must be   **161 when . . . for** when
I'm ready for you (i.e., never)   **169 Go to** (An expression of remon-
strance.)   **186 your way** i.e., the way you should think of her
190 invention imagination

IAGO   She's the worse for all this.

OTHELLO   O, a thousand, a thousand times! And then, of so gentle a condition!   193

IAGO   Ay, too gentle.   194

OTHELLO   Nay, that's certain. But yet the pity of it, Iago! O, Iago, the pity of it, Iago!

IAGO   If you are so fond over her iniquity, give her patent   197 to offend, for if it touch not you it comes near nobody.

OTHELLO   I will chop her into messes. Cuckold me?   199

IAGO   O, 'tis foul in her.

OTHELLO   With mine officer?

IAGO   That's fouler.

OTHELLO   Get me some poison, Iago, this night. I'll not expostulate with her, lest her body and beauty un-   204 provide my mind again. This night, Iago.   205

IAGO   Do it not with poison. Strangle her in her bed, even the bed she hath contaminated.

OTHELLO   Good, good! The justice of it pleases. Very good.

IAGO   And for Cassio, let me be his undertaker. You   209 shall hear more by midnight.

OTHELLO
Excellent good. [*A trumpet within.*] What trumpet is that same?

IAGO   I warrant, something from Venice.

Enter Lodovico, Desdemona, and attendants.

'Tis Lodovico. This comes from the Duke.
See, your wife's with him.

LODOVICO
God save you, worthy General!

OTHELLO   With all my heart, sir.   215

LODOVICO [*Giving him a letter*]
The Duke and the senators of Venice greet you.

OTHELLO
I kiss the instrument of their pleasures.
                    [*He opens the letter, and reads.*]

___

193 gentle a condition wellborn and wellbred   **194 gentle** generous, yielding (to other men)   **197 fond** foolish.   **patent** license   **199 messes** portions of meat, i.e., bits   **204–205 unprovide** weaken, render unfit   **209 be his undertaker** undertake to dispatch him   **215 With all my heart** i.e., I thank you most heartily

DESDEMONA
  And what's the news, good cousin Lodovico?
IAGO
  I am very glad to see you, signor.
  Welcome to Cyprus.
LODOVICO
  I thank you. How does Lieutenant Cassio?
IAGO Lives, sir.
DESDEMONA
  Cousin, there's fall'n between him and my lord
  An unkind breach; but you shall make all well.   224
OTHELLO Are you sure of that?
DESDEMONA My lord?
OTHELLO [*Reads*] "This fail you not to do, as you will—"
LODOVICO
  He did not call; he's busy in the paper.
  Is there division twixt my lord and Cassio?
DESDEMONA
  A most unhappy one. I would do much
  T' atone them, for the love I bear to Cassio.   231
OTHELLO Fire and brimstone!
DESDEMONA My lord?
OTHELLO Are you wise?
DESDEMONA
  What, is he angry?
LODOVICO   Maybe the letter moved him;
  For, as I think, they do command him home,
  Deputing Cassio in his government.   237
DESDEMONA By my troth, I am glad on 't.   238
OTHELLO Indeed?
DESDEMONA My lord?
OTHELLO I am glad to see you mad.   241
DESDEMONA Why, sweet Othello—
OTHELLO [*Striking her*] Devil!
DESDEMONA I have not deserved this.
LODOVICO
  My lord, this would not be believed in Venice,

---

224 unkind unnatural, contrary to their natures; hurtful **231 atone**
reconcile **237 government** office **238 on 't** of it **241 I am ... mad**
i.e., I am glad to see that you are insane enough to rejoice in Cassio's
promotion (? Othello bitterly plays on Desdemona's *I am glad*.)

Though I should swear I saw 't. 'Tis very much.   246
Make her amends; she weeps.
OTHELLO   O devil, devil!
If that the earth could teem with woman's tears,   248
Each drop she falls would prove a crocodile.   249
Out of my sight!
DESDEMONA   I will not stay to offend you. [*Going.*]
LODOVICO Truly, an obedient lady.
I do beseech your lordship, call her back.
OTHELLO Mistress!
DESDEMONA [*Returning*] My lord?
OTHELLO What would you with her, sir?   255
LODOVICO Who, I, my lord?
OTHELLO
Ay, you did wish that I would make her turn.
Sir, she can turn, and turn, and yet go on
And turn again; and she can weep, sir, weep;
And she's obedient, as you say, obedient,   260
Very obedient.—Proceed you in your tears.—
Concerning this, sir—O well-painted passion!—   262
I am commanded home.—Get you away;
I'll send for you anon.—Sir, I obey the mandate
And will return to Venice.—Hence, avaunt!
                              [*Exit Desdemona.*]
Cassio shall have my place. And, sir, tonight
I do entreat that we may sup together.
You are welcome, sir, to Cyprus.—Goats and monkeys! 268
                                        Exit.
LODOVICO
Is this the noble Moor whom our full Senate
Call all in all sufficient? Is this the nature
Whom passion could not shake? Whose solid virtue
The shot of accident nor dart of chance
Could neither graze nor pierce?
IAGO   He is much changed.

---

246 very much too much, outrageous **248 teem** breed, be impreg-
nated **249 falls** lets fall. **crocodile** (Crocodiles were supposed to weep
hypocritical tears for their victims.) **255 What . . . sir** (Othello implies
that Desdemona is pliant and will do a *turn*, ll. 257–259, for any man.)
260 obedient (with much the same sexual connotation as *turn* in
ll. 257–259) **262 passion** i.e., grief **268 Goats and monkeys** (See
3.3.419.)

LODOVICO
  Are his wits safe? Is he not light of brain?
IAGO
  He's that he is. I may not breathe my censure   275
  What he might be. If what he might he is not,   276
  I would to heaven he were!
LODOVICO   What, strike his wife?   277
IAGO
  Faith, that was not so well; yet would I knew
  That stroke would prove the worst!
LODOVICO   Is it his use?   279
  Or did the letters work upon his blood   280
  And new-create his fault?
IAGO   Alas, alas!
  It is not honesty in me to speak
  What I have seen and known. You shall observe him,
  And his own courses will denote him so
  That I may save my speech. Do but go after,
  And mark how he continues.
LODOVICO
  I am sorry that I am deceived in him.   *Exeunt.*

❖

4.2   *Enter Othello and Emilia.*

OTHELLO You have seen nothing then?
EMILIA
  Nor ever heard, nor ever did suspect.
OTHELLO
  Yes, you have seen Cassio and she together.
EMILIA
  But then I saw no harm, and then I heard
  Each syllable that breath made up between them.
OTHELLO What, did they never whisper?
EMILIA Never, my lord.
OTHELLO Nor send you out o' the way?

275-277 I may . . . were i.e., I dare not venture an opinion as to whether he's of unsound mind, as you suggest; but if he isn't, then it might be better to wish he were in fact insane, since only that could excuse his wild behavior **279 use** custom **280 blood** passions

4.2. Location: The citadel.

EMILIA Never.

OTHELLO
  To fetch her fan, her gloves, her mask, nor nothing?

EMILIA Never, my lord.

OTHELLO That's strange.

EMILIA
  I durst, my lord, to wager she is honest,
  Lay down my soul at stake. If you think other,   14
  Remove your thought; it doth abuse your bosom.
  If any wretch have put this in your head,
  Let heaven requite it with the serpent's curse!   17
  For if she be not honest, chaste, and true,
  There's no man happy; the purest of their wives
  Is foul as slander.

OTHELLO   Bid her come hither. Go.

                                    Exit Emilia.

  She says enough; yet she's a simple bawd   21
  That cannot say as much. This is a subtle whore,   22
  A closet lock and key of villainous secrets.   23
  And yet she'll kneel and pray; I have seen her do 't.

      Enter Desdemona and Emilia.

DESDEMONA My lord, what is your will?

OTHELLO Pray you, chuck, come hither.

DESDEMONA
  What is your pleasure?

OTHELLO   Let me see your eyes.
  Look in my face.

DESDEMONA   What horrible fancy's this?

OTHELLO [*To Emilia*] Some of your function, mistress.   29
  Leave procreants alone and shut the door;   30
  Cough or cry "hem" if anybody come.
  Your mystery, your mystery! Nay, dispatch.   32

                                    Exit Emilia.

---

14 at stake as the wager **17 the serpent's curse** the curse pronounced
by God on the serpent for deceiving Eve, just as some man has done to
Othello and Desdemona. (See Genesis 3:14.) **21–22 she's . . . much** i.e.,
any procuress or go-between who couldn't make up as convincing a
story as Emilia's would have to be pretty stupid **22 This** i.e., Desdemona **23 closet lock and key** i.e., concealer **29 Some . . . function** i.e.,
practice your chosen profession, that of bawd (by guarding the door)
30 procreants mating couples **32 mystery** trade, occupation

DESDEMONA [*Kneeling*]
  Upon my knees, what doth your speech import?
  I understand a fury in your words,
  But not the words.
OTHELLO
  Why, what art thou?
DESDEMONA   Your wife, my lord, your true
  And loyal wife.
OTHELLO   Come, swear it, damn thyself,
  Lest, being like one of heaven, the devils themselves   38
  Should fear to seize thee. Therefore be double damned:
  Swear thou art honest.
DESDEMONA   Heaven doth truly know it.
OTHELLO
  Heaven truly knows that thou art false as hell.
DESDEMONA
  To whom, my lord? With whom? How am I false?
OTHELLO [*Weeping*]
  Ah, Desdemon! Away, away, away!
DESDEMONA
  Alas the heavy day! Why do you weep?
  Am I the motive of these tears, my lord?   45
  If haply you my father do suspect
  An instrument of this your calling back,
  Lay not your blame on me. If you have lost him,
  I have lost him too.
OTHELLO   Had it pleased heaven
  To try me with affliction, had they rained   50
  All kinds of sores and shames on my bare head,
  Steeped me in poverty to the very lips,
  Given to captivity me and my utmost hopes,
  I should have found in some place of my soul
  A drop of patience. But, alas, to make me
  A fixèd figure for the time of scorn   56
  To point his slow and moving finger at!   57
  Yet could I bear that too, well, very well.

38 being . . . heaven looking like an angel   **45 motive** cause   **50 they**
i.e., heavenly powers   **56 time of scorn** i.e., scornful world   **57 his** its.
slow and moving finger i.e., hour hand of the clock, moving so slowly it
seems hardly to move at all. (Othello envisages himself as being eternally pointed at by the scornful world as the numbers on a clock are
pointed at by the hour hand.)

But there where I have garnered up my heart,   59
Where either I must live or bear no life,
The fountain from the which my current runs   61
Or else dries up—to be discarded thence!
Or keep it as a cistern for foul toads   63
To knot and gender in! Turn thy complexion there,   64
Patience, thou young and rose-lipped cherubin—   65
Ay, there look grim as hell!   66

DESDEMONA

I hope my noble lord esteems me honest.   67

OTHELLO

O, ay, as summer flies are in the shambles,   68
That quicken even with blowing. O thou weed,   69
Who art so lovely fair and smell'st so sweet
That the sense aches at thee, would thou hadst ne'er
        been born!

DESDEMONA

Alas, what ignorant sin have I committed?   72

OTHELLO

Was this fair paper, this most goodly book,
Made to write "whore" upon? What committed?
Committed? O thou public commoner!   75
I should make very forges of my cheeks,
That would to cinders burn up modesty,
Did I but speak thy deeds. What committed?
Heaven stops the nose at it and the moon winks;   79
The bawdy wind, that kisses all it meets,   80
Is hushed within the hollow mine of earth   81
And will not hear 't. What committed?
Impudent strumpet!

DESDEMONA   By heaven, you do me wrong.

OTHELLO   Are not you a strumpet?

DESDEMONA   No, as I am a Christian.

---

59 garnered stored   **61 fountain** spring   **63 cistern** cesspool   **64 knot**
i.e., couple.   **gender** engender.   **Turn . . . there** change your color, grow
pale, at such a sight   **65–66 Patience . . . hell** (Even Patience, that rose-
lipped cherub, will look grim and pale at this spectacle.)   **67 honest**
chaste   **68 shambles** slaughterhouse   **69 quicken** come to life.   **with
blowing** i.e., with the puffing up of something rotten in which maggots
are breeding   **72 ignorant sin** sin in ignorance   **75 commoner** prostitute   **79 winks** closes her eyes. (The moon symbolizes chastity.)
80 bawdy kissing one and all   **81 mine** cave (where the winds were
thought to dwell)

If to preserve this vessel for my lord 86
From any other foul unlawful touch
Be not to be a strumpet, I am none.

OTHELLO What, not a whore?

DESDEMONA No, as I shall be saved.

OTHELLO Is 't possible?

DESDEMONA
O, heaven forgive us!

OTHELLO   I cry you mercy, then. 92
I took you for that cunning whore of Venice
That married with Othello. [*Calling out.*] You, mistress,
That have the office opposite to Saint Peter
And keep the gate of hell!

      Enter Emilia.

                              You, you, ay, you!
We have done our course. There's money for your
      pains.   [*He gives money.*] 97
I pray you, turn the key and keep our counsel.   *Exit.*

EMILIA
Alas, what does this gentleman conceive? 99
How do you, madam? How do you, my good lady?

DESDEMONA Faith, half asleep. 101

EMILIA
Good madam, what's the matter with my lord?

DESDEMONA With who?

EMILIA Why, with my lord, madam.

DESDEMONA
Who is thy lord?

EMILIA   He that is yours, sweet lady.

DESDEMONA
I have none. Do not talk to me, Emilia.
I cannot weep, nor answers have I none
But what should go by water. Prithee, tonight 108
Lay on my bed my wedding sheets, remember;
And call thy husband hither.

EMILIA   Here's a change indeed!   *Exit.*

---

86 vessel i.e., body   **92 cry you mercy** beg your pardon   **97 course**
business (with an indecent suggestion of "trick," turn at sex)
99 conceive suppose, think   **101 half asleep** i.e., dazed   **108 go by
water** be expressed by tears

DESDEMONA
  'Tis meet I should be used so, very meet.   112
  How have I been behaved, that he might stick   113
  The small'st opinion on my least misuse?   114

      Enter Iago and Emilia.

IAGO
  What is your pleasure, madam? How is 't with you?
DESDEMONA
  I cannot tell. Those that do teach young babes
  Do it with gentle means and easy tasks.
  He might have chid me so, for, in good faith,
  I am a child to chiding.
IAGO   What is the matter, lady?
EMILIA
  Alas, Iago, my lord hath so bewhored her,
  Thrown such despite and heavy terms upon her,
  That true hearts cannot bear it.
DESDEMONA   Am I that name, Iago?
IAGO   What name, fair lady?
DESDEMONA
  Such as she said my lord did say I was.
EMILIA
  He called her whore. A beggar in his drink
  Could not have laid such terms upon his callet.   128
IAGO   Why did he so?
DESDEMONA [*Weeping*]
  I do not know. I am sure I am none such.
IAGO   Do not weep, do not weep. Alas the day!
EMILIA
  Hath she forsook so many noble matches,
  Her father and her country and her friends,
  To be called whore? Would it not make one weep?
DESDEMONA
  It is my wretched fortune.
IAGO   Beshrew him for 't!   135
  How comes this trick upon him?
DESDEMONA   Nay, heaven doth know. 136

112 **meet** fitting   113 **stick** attach   114 **opinion** censure.   **least misuse**
slightest misconduct   128 **callet** whore   135 **Beshrew** curse   136 **trick**
strange behavior, delusion

EMILIA

I will be hanged if some eternal villain,   137
Some busy and insinuating rogue,   138
Some cogging, cozening slave, to get some office,   139
Have not devised this slander. I will be hanged else.

IAGO

Fie, there is no such man. It is impossible.

DESDEMONA

If any such there be, heaven pardon him!

EMILIA

A halter pardon him! And hell gnaw his bones!   143
Why should he call her whore? Who keeps her
    company?
What place? What time? What form? What likelihood?   145
The Moor's abused by some most villainous knave,
Some base notorious knave, some scurvy fellow.
O heavens, that such companions thou'dst unfold,   148
And put in every honest hand a whip
To lash the rascals naked through the world
Even from the east to th' west!

IAGO   Speak within door.   151

EMILIA

O, fie upon them! Some such squire he was   152
That turned your wit the seamy side without   153
And made you to suspect me with the Moor.

IAGO

You are a fool. Go to.

DESDEMONA   Alas, Iago,   155
What shall I do to win my lord again?
Good friend, go to him; for, by this light of heaven,
I know not how I lost him. Here I kneel. [*She kneels.*]
If e'er my will did trespass 'gainst his love,
Either in discourse of thought or actual deed,   160
Or that mine eyes, mine ears, or any sense   161
Delighted them in any other form;   162

---

137 eternal inveterate **138 insinuating** ingratiating, fawning, whee-
dling **139 cogging** cheating. **cozening** defrauding **143 halter** hangman's noose **145 form** appearance, circumstance **148 companions**
fellows. **unfold** expose **151 within door** i.e., not so loud **152 squire**
fellow **153 seamy side without** wrong side out **155 Go to** i.e., that's
enough **160 discourse of thought** process of thinking **161 that** if (also
in l. 163) **162 Delighted them** took delight

Or that I do not yet, and ever did,   163
And ever will—though he do shake me off
To beggarly divorcement—love him dearly,
Comfort forswear me! Unkindness may do much,   166
And his unkindness may defeat my life,   167
But never taint my love. I cannot say "whore."
It does abhor me now I speak the word;   169
To do the act that might the addition earn   170
Not the world's mass of vanity could make me.   171

IAGO
I pray you, be content. 'Tis but his humor.   172
The business of the state does him offense,
And he does chide with you.

DESDEMONA   If 'twere no other—

IAGO   It is but so, I warrant.   [*Trumpets within.*]
Hark, how these instruments summon you to supper!
The messengers of Venice stays the meat.   178
Go in, and weep not. All things shall be well.
                    Exeunt Desdemona and Emilia.

    Enter Roderigo.

How now, Roderigo?

RODERIGO   I do not find that thou deal'st justly with me.

IAGO   What in the contrary?

RODERIGO   Every day thou daff'st me with some device,   183
    Iago, and rather, as it seems to me now, keep'st from
    me all conveniency than suppliest me with the least   185
    advantage of hope. I will indeed no longer endure it,   186
    nor am I yet persuaded to put up in peace what al-   187
    ready I have foolishly suffered.

IAGO   Will you hear me, Roderigo?

RODERIGO   Faith, I have heard too much, for your words
    and performances are no kin together.

IAGO   You charge me most unjustly.

RODERIGO   With naught but truth. I have wasted myself
    out of my means. The jewels you have had from me to

163 **yet** still   166 **Comfort forswear** may heavenly comfort forsake
167 **defeat** destroy   169 **abhor** (1) fill me with abhorrence (2) make me
whorelike   170 **addition** title   171 **vanity** showy splendor   172 **humor**
mood   178 **stays the meat** are waiting to dine   183 **thou daff'st me** you
put me off.   **device** excuse, trick   185 **conveniency** advantage, opportunity   186 **advantage** increase   187 **put up** submit to, tolerate

deliver Desdemona would half have corrupted a vo- 195
tarist. You have told me she hath received them and 196
returned me expectations and comforts of sudden re- 197
spect and acquaintance, but I find none. 198

IAGO Well, go to, very well.

RODERIGO "Very well"! "Go to"! I cannot go to, man, nor 200
'tis not very well. By this hand, I think it is scurvy, and
begin to find myself fopped in it. 202

IAGO Very well.

RODERIGO I tell you 'tis not very well. I will make myself 204
known to Desdemona. If she will return me my jewels,
I will give over my suit and repent my unlawful solic-
itation; if not, assure yourself I will seek satisfaction 207
of you.

IAGO You have said now? 209

RODERIGO Ay, and said nothing but what I protest in- 210
tendment of doing. 211

IAGO Why, now I see there's mettle in thee, and even
from this instant do build on thee a better opinion
than ever before. Give me thy hand, Roderigo. Thou
hast taken against me a most just exception; but yet I
protest I have dealt most directly in thy affair.

RODERIGO It hath not appeared.

IAGO I grant indeed it hath not appeared, and your suspicion is not without wit and judgment. But, Roderigo, if thou hast that in thee indeed which I have
greater reason to believe now than ever—I mean purpose, courage, and valor—this night show it. If thou
the next night following enjoy not Desdemona, take
me from this world with treachery and devise engines 224
for my life. 225

RODERIGO Well, what is it? Is it within reason and compass?

---

195 deliver deliver to   **195–196 votarist** nun   **197–198 sudden respect**
immediate consideration   **200 I cannot go to** (Roderigo changes Iago's
go to, an expression urging patience, to *I cannot go to,* "I have no
opportunity for sex.")   **202 fopped** fooled, duped   **204 not very well**
(Roderigo changes Iago's *very well,* "all right, then," to *not very well,*
"not at all good.")   **207 satisfaction** repayment. (The term normally
means the settling of accounts in a duel.)   **209 You . . . now** have you
finished   **210–211 intendment** intention   **224–225 engines for** plots
against

IAGO Sir, there is especial commission come from Venice to depute Cassio in Othello's place.

RODERIGO Is that true? Why, then Othello and Desdemona return again to Venice.

IAGO O, no; he goes into Mauritania and takes away
with him the fair Desdemona, unless his abode be
lingered here by some accident; wherein none can be
so determinate as the removing of Cassio.   235

RODERIGO How do you mean, removing of him?

IAGO Why, by making him uncapable of Othello's
place—knocking out his brains.

RODERIGO And that you would have me to do?

IAGO Ay, if you dare do yourself a profit and a right.
He sups tonight with a harlotry, and thither will I go 241
to him. He knows not yet of his honorable fortune. If
you will watch his going thence, which I will fashion
to fall out between twelve and one, you may take him 244
at your pleasure. I will be near to second your attempt,
and he shall fall between us. Come, stand not amazed
at it, but go along with me. I will show you such a
necessity in his death that you shall think yourself
bound to put it on him. It is now high suppertime,   249
and the night grows to waste. About it.   250

RODERIGO I will hear further reason for this.

IAGO And you shall be satisfied.   *Exeunt.*

❖

4.3   *Enter Othello, Lodovico, Desdemona, Emilia,
and attendants.*

LODOVICO
I do beseech you, sir, trouble yourself no further.

OTHELLO
O, pardon me; 'twill do me good to walk.

LODOVICO
Madam, good night. I humbly thank your ladyship.

---

235 determinate effective   **241 harlotry** slut   **244 fall out** occur
249 high fully   **250 grows to waste** wastes away
4.3. Location: The citadel.

DESDEMONA

Your honor is most welcome.

OTHELLO   Will you walk, sir?

O, Desdemona!

DESDEMONA   My lord?

OTHELLO   Get you to bed on th' instant. I will be returned forthwith. Dismiss your attendant there. Look 't
be done.

DESDEMONA   I will, my lord.

                Exit [Othello, with Lodovico and attendants].

EMILIA   How goes it now? He looks gentler than he did.

DESDEMONA

He says he will return incontinent,   12

And hath commanded me to go to bed,

And bid me to dismiss you.

EMILIA   Dismiss me?

DESDEMONA

It was his bidding. Therefore, good Emilia,

Give me my nightly wearing, and adieu.

We must not now displease him.

EMILIA   I would you had never seen him!

DESDEMONA

So would not I. My love doth so approve him

That even his stubbornness, his checks, his frowns—   21

Prithee, unpin me—have grace and favor in them.

                [Emilia prepares Desdemona for bed.]

EMILIA   I have laid those sheets you bade me on the
bed.

DESDEMONA

All's one. Good faith, how foolish are our minds!   25

If I do die before thee, prithee shroud me

In one of these same sheets.

EMILIA   Come, come, you talk.   27

DESDEMONA

My mother had a maid called Barbary.

She was in love, and he she loved proved mad   29

And did forsake her. She had a song of "Willow."

An old thing 'twas, but it expressed her fortune,

12 **incontinent** immediately   21 **stubbornness** roughness.   **checks**
rebukes   25 **All's one** all right. It doesn't really matter   27 **talk** i.e.,
prattle   29 **mad** wild, i.e., faithless

And she died singing it. That song tonight
Will not go from my mind; I have much to do   33
But to go hang my head all at one side   34
And sing it like poor Barbary. Prithee, dispatch.
EMILIA Shall I go fetch your nightgown?   36
DESDEMONA No, unpin me here.
    This Lodovico is a proper man.   38
EMILIA A very handsome man.
DESDEMONA He speaks well.
EMILIA I know a lady in Venice would have walked
    barefoot to Palestine for a touch of his nether lip.
DESDEMONA [*Singing*]
        "The poor soul sat sighing by a sycamore tree,
            Sing all a green willow;   44
        Her hand on her bosom, her head on her knee,
            Sing willow, willow, willow.
        The fresh streams ran by her and murmured her
            moans;
            Sing willow, willow, willow;
        Her salt tears fell from her, and softened the
            stones—"
    Lay by these.
    [*Singing*.] "Sing willow, willow, willow—"
    Prithee, hie thee. He'll come anon.   52
    [*Singing*.] "Sing all a green willow must be my garland.
        Let nobody blame him; his scorn I approve—"
    Nay, that's not next.—Hark! Who is 't that knocks?
EMILIA It's the wind.
DESDEMONA [*Singing*]
        "I called my love false love; but what said he then?
            Sing willow, willow, willow;
        If I court more women, you'll couch with more
            men."
    So, get thee gone. Good night. Mine eyes do itch;
    Doth that bode weeping?
EMILIA   'Tis neither here nor there.

33–34 I . . . hang I can scarcely keep myself from hanging
36 nightgown dressing gown **38 proper** handsome **44 willow** (A
conventional emblem of disappointed love.) **52 hie thee** hurry. **anon**
right away

DESDEMONA
I have heard it said so. O, these men, these men!
Dost thou in conscience think—tell me, Emilia—
That there be women do abuse their husbands   64
In such gross kind?
EMILIA   There be some such, no question.
DESDEMONA
Wouldst thou do such a deed for all the world?
EMILIA
Why, would not you?
DESDEMONA   No, by this heavenly light!
EMILIA
Nor I neither by this heavenly light;
I might do 't as well i' the dark.
DESDEMONA
Wouldst thou do such a deed for all the world?
EMILIA
The world's a huge thing. It is a great price
For a small vice.
DESDEMONA
Good troth, I think thou wouldst not.
EMILIA   By my troth, I think I should, and undo 't when
I had done. Marry, I would not do such a thing for a
joint ring, nor for measures of lawn, nor for gowns, 76
petticoats, nor caps, nor any petty exhibition. But for 77
all the whole world! Uds pity, who would not make 78
her husband a cuckold to make him a monarch? I
should venture purgatory for 't.
DESDEMONA
Beshrew me if I would do such a wrong
For the whole world.
EMILIA   Why, the wrong is but a wrong i' the world, and
having the world for your labor, 'tis a wrong in your
own world, and you might quickly make it right.
DESDEMONA
I do not think there is any such woman.
EMILIA   Yes, a dozen, and as many

---

64 abuse deceive   **76 joint ring** a ring made in separate halves.   **lawn**
fine linen   **77 exhibition** gift   **78 Uds** i.e., God's

To th' vantage as would store the world they played for. 88
But I do think it is their husbands' faults
If wives do fall. Say that they slack their duties 90
And pour our treasures into foreign laps, 91
Or else break out in peevish jealousies,
Throwing restraint upon us? Or say they strike us, 93
Or scant our former having in despite? 94
Why, we have galls, and though we have some grace, 95
Yet have we some revenge. Let husbands know
Their wives have sense like them. They see, and smell, 97
And have their palates both for sweet and sour,
As husbands have. What is it that they do
When they change us for others? Is it sport? 100
I think it is. And doth affection breed it? 101
I think it doth. Is 't frailty that thus errs?
It is so too. And have not we affections,
Desires for sport, and frailty, as men have?
Then let them use us well; else let them know,
The ills we do, their ills instruct us so.

DESDEMONA
Good night, good night. God me such uses send 107
Not to pick bad from bad, but by bad mend! 108

Exeunt.

❖

88 **To th' vantage** in addition, to boot. **store** populate. **played**
(1) gambled (2) sported sexually 90 **duties** marital duties 91 **pour . . .
laps** i.e., are unfaithful, give what is rightfully ours (semen) to other
women 93 **Throwing . . . us** i.e., jealously restricting our freedom to
see other men 94 **scant . . . despite** reduce our allowance to spite us
95 **have galls** i.e., are capable of resenting injury and insult 97 **sense**
physical sense 100 **sport** sexual pastime 101 **affection** passion
107 **uses** habit, practice 108 **Not . . . mend** i.e., not to learn bad conduct from others' badness (as Emilia has suggested women learn from
men), but to mend my ways by perceiving what badness is, making
spiritual benefit out of evil and adversity

5.1   *Enter Iago and Roderigo.*

IAGO

Here stand behind this bulk. Straight will he come.   1
Wear thy good rapier bare, and put it home.   2
Quick, quick! Fear nothing. I'll be at thy elbow.
It makes us or it mars us. Think on that,
And fix most firm thy resolution.

RODERIGO

Be near at hand. I may miscarry in 't.

IAGO

Here, at thy hand. Be bold, and take thy stand.
[Iago stands aside. Roderigo conceals himself.]

RODERIGO

I have no great devotion to the deed;
And yet he hath given me satisfying reasons.
'Tis but a man gone. Forth, my sword! He dies.
[He draws.]

IAGO

I have rubbed this young quat almost to the sense,   11
And he grows angry. Now, whether he kill Cassio
Or Cassio him, or each do kill the other,
Every way makes my gain. Live Roderigo,   14
He calls me to a restitution large
Of gold and jewels that I bobbed from him   16
As gifts to Desdemona.
It must not be. If Cassio do remain,
He hath a daily beauty in his life
That makes me ugly; and besides, the Moor
May unfold me to him; there stand I in much peril.   21
No, he must die. Be 't so. I hear him coming.

Enter Cassio.

RODERIGO *[Coming forth]*

I know his gait, 'tis he.—Villain, thou diest!
[He makes a pass at Cassio.]

CASSIO

That thrust had been mine enemy indeed,

5.1. Location: A street in Cyprus.
1 bulk framework projecting from the front of a shop   **2 bare** un-
sheathed   **11 quat** pimple, pustule.   **to the sense** to the quick   **14 Live
Roderigo** if Roderigo live   **16 bobbed** swindled   **21 unfold** expose

But that my coat is better than thou know'st.   25
I will make proof of thine.
                         [*He draws, and wounds Roderigo.*]
RODERIGO   O, I am slain!   [*He falls.*] 26
                         [*Iago from behind wounds Cassio
                              in the leg, and exit.*]

CASSIO
I am maimed forever. Help, ho! Murder! Murder!

     Enter Othello.

OTHELLO
The voice of Cassio! Iago keeps his word.
RODERIGO   O, villain that I am!
OTHELLO   It is even so.
CASSIO   O, help, ho! Light! A surgeon!
OTHELLO
'Tis he. O brave Iago, honest and just,
That hast such noble sense of thy friend's wrong!
Thou teachest me. Minion, your dear lies dead,   34
And your unblest fate hies. Strumpet, I come.   35
Forth of my heart those charms, thine eyes, are blotted; 36
Thy bed, lust-stained, shall with lust's blood be spotted.
                              Exit Othello.

     Enter Lodovico and Gratiano.

CASSIO
What ho! No watch? No passage? Murder! Murder!   38
GRATIANO
'Tis some mischance. The voice is very direful.
CASSIO   O, help!
LODOVICO   Hark!
RODERIGO   O wretched villain!
LODOVICO
Two or three groan. 'Tis heavy night;   43
These may be counterfeits. Let's think 't unsafe
To come in to the cry without more help.   45
                    [*They remain near the entrance.*]

25 coat (Possibly a garment of mail under the outer clothing, or simply
a tougher coat than Roderigo expected.)   **26 proof** a test   **34 Minion**
hussy (i.e., Desdemona)   **35 hies** hastens on   **36 Forth of** from out
38 passage people passing by   **43 heavy** thick, dark   **45 come in to**
approach

RODERIGO
Nobody come? Then shall I bleed to death.

Enter Iago [in his shirtsleeves, with a light].

LODOVICO Hark!

GRATIANO
Here's one comes in his shirt, with light and weapons.

IAGO
Who's there? Whose noise is this that cries on murder? 49

LODOVICO
We do not know.

IAGO   Did not you hear a cry?

CASSIO
Here, here! For heaven's sake, help me!

IAGO   What's the matter?
                                          [*He moves toward Cassio.*]

GRATIANO [*To Lodovico*]
This is Othello's ancient, as I take it.

LODOVICO [*To Gratiano*]
The same indeed, a very valiant fellow.

IAGO [*To Cassio*]
What are you here that cry so grievously? 54

CASSIO
Iago? O, I am spoiled, undone by villains! 55
Give me some help.

IAGO
O me, Lieutenant! What villains have done this?

CASSIO
I think that one of them is hereabout,
And cannot make away.

IAGO   O treacherous villains! 59
[*To Lodovico and Gratiano.*] What are you there? Come
   in, and give some help.   [*They advance.*]

RODERIGO O, help me there!

CASSIO
That's one of them.

IAGO   O murderous slave! O villain!
                              [*He stabs Roderigo.*]

RODERIGO
O damned Iago! O inhuman dog!

49 **cries on** cries out 54 **What** who (also at ll. 60 and 66) 55 **spoiled**
ruined, done for 59 **make** get

IAGO
  Kill men i' the dark?—Where be these bloody thieves?—
  How silent is this town!—Ho! Murder, murder!—
  [*To Lodovico and Gratiano.*] What may you be? Are you
    of good or evil?
LODOVICO As you shall prove us, praise us.   67
IAGO Signor Lodovico?
LODOVICO He, sir.
IAGO
  I cry you mercy. Here's Cassio hurt by villains.   70
GRATIANO Cassio?
IAGO How is 't, brother?
CASSIO My leg is cut in two.
IAGO Marry, heaven forbid!
  Light, gentlemen! I'll bind it with my shirt.
                    [*He hands them the light, and tends
                              to Cassio's wound.*]

      Enter Bianca.

BIANCA
  What is the matter, ho? Who is 't that cried?
IAGO Who is 't that cried?
BIANCA   O my dear Cassio!
  My sweet Cassio! O Cassio, Cassio, Cassio!
IAGO
  O notable strumpet! Cassio, may you suspect
  Who they should be that have thus mangled you?
CASSIO No.
GRATIANO
  I am sorry to find you thus. I have been to seek you.
IAGO
  Lend me a garter. [*He applies a tourniquet.*] So.—O,
    for a chair,   83
  To bear him easily hence!
BIANCA
  Alas, he faints! O Cassio, Cassio, Cassio!
IAGO
  Gentlemen all, I do suspect this trash
  To be a party in this injury.—
  Patience awhile, good Cassio.—Come, come;

67 praise appraise **70 I cry you mercy** I beg your pardon **83 chair**
litter

Lend me a light. [*He shines the light on Roderigo.*] Know
  we this face or no?
Alas, my friend and my dear countryman
Roderigo! No.—Yes, sure.—O heaven! Roderigo!
GRATIANO   What, of Venice?
IAGO   Even he, sir. Did you know him?
GRATIANO   Know him? Ay.
IAGO
  Signor Gratiano? I cry your gentle pardon.   95
  These bloody accidents must excuse my manners   96
  That so neglected you.
GRATIANO   I am glad to see you.
IAGO
  How do you, Cassio? O, a chair, a chair!
GRATIANO   Roderigo!
IAGO
  He, he, 'tis he. [*A litter is brought in.*] O, that's well said;
    the chair.   100
  Some good man bear him carefully from hence;
  I'll fetch the General's surgeon. [*To Bianca.*] For you,
    mistress,
  Save you your labor.—He that lies slain here, Cassio,   103
  Was my dear friend. What malice was between you?   104
CASSIO
  None in the world, nor do I know the man.
IAGO [*To Bianca*]
  What, look you pale?—O, bear him out o' th' air.   106
                   [*Cassio and Roderigo are borne off.*]
  Stay you, good gentlemen.—Look you pale, mistress?—   107
  Do you perceive the gastness of her eye?—   108
  Nay, if you stare, we shall hear more anon.—   109
  Behold her well; I pray you, look upon her.
  Do you see, gentlemen? Nay, guiltiness
  Will speak, though tongues were out of use.

      [*Enter Emilia.*]

95 gentle noble   96 accidents sudden events   100 well said well done
103 Save . . . labor i.e., never you mind tending Cassio   104 malice
enmity   106 bear . . . air (Fresh air was thought to be dangerous for a
wound.)   107 Stay you (Lodovico and Gratiano are evidently about to
leave.)   108 gastness terror   109 stare (Iago pretends to interpret
Bianca's wild looks as an involuntary confession of guilt.)

EMILIA
    'Las, what's the matter? What's the matter, husband?
IAGO
    Cassio hath here been set on in the dark
    By Roderigo and fellows that are scaped.
    He's almost slain, and Roderigo dead.
EMILIA
    Alas, good gentleman! Alas, good Cassio!
IAGO
    This is the fruits of whoring. Prithee, Emilia,
    Go know of Cassio where he supped tonight.   119
    [*To Bianca.*] What, do you shake at that?
BIANCA
    He supped at my house, but I therefore shake not.
IAGO
    O, did he so? I charge you go with me.
EMILIA   O, fie upon thee, strumpet!
BIANCA
    I am no strumpet, but of life as honest   124
    As you that thus abuse me.
EMILIA   As I? Faugh! Fie upon thee!
IAGO
    Kind gentlemen, let's go see poor Cassio dressed.—   127
    Come, mistress, you must tell 's another tale.
    Emilia, run you to the citadel
    And tell my lord and lady what hath happed.—
    Will you go on afore? [*Aside.*] This is the night
    That either makes me or fordoes me quite.   *Exeunt.* 132

✦

5.2   *Enter Othello [with a light], and Desdemona in*
    her bed.

OTHELLO
    It is the cause, it is the cause, my soul.   1
    Let me not name it to you, you chaste stars!
    It is the cause. Yet I'll not shed her blood,

119 know learn   **124 honest** chaste   **127 Cassio dressed** Cassio's
wounds dressed   **132 fordoes** undoes, ruins

5.2. Location: A bedchamber in the citadel.
s.d. in her bed (The bed is presumably "thrust out" onstage as the
scene begins.)   **1 cause** i.e., cause of justice, the offense itself, which
Othello must correct as an agent of justice

Nor scar that whiter skin of hers than snow,
And smooth as monumental alabaster.   5
Yet she must die, else she'll betray more men.
Put out the light, and then put out the light.   7
If I quench thee, thou flaming minister,   8
I can again thy former light restore,
Should I repent me; but once put out thy light,   10
Thou cunning'st pattern of excelling nature,   11
I know not where is that Promethean heat   12
That can thy light relume. When I have plucked thy rose,   13
I cannot give it vital growth again;
It needs must wither. I'll smell thee on the tree.

                                [He kisses her.]

O balmy breath, that dost almost persuade
Justice to break her sword! One more, one more.
Be thus when thou art dead, and I will kill thee,
And love thee after. One more, and that's the last.

                                [He kisses her.]

So sweet was ne'er so fatal. I must weep,
But they are cruel tears. This sorrow's heavenly;   21
It strikes where it doth love. She wakes.   22

DESDEMONA Who's there? Othello?

OTHELLO Ay, Desdemona.

DESDEMONA Will you come to bed, my lord?

OTHELLO Have you prayed tonight, Desdemon?

DESDEMONA Ay, my lord.

OTHELLO

If you bethink yourself of any crime   28
Unreconciled as yet to heaven and grace,
Solicit for it straight.   30

DESDEMONA

Alack, my lord, what may you mean by that?

OTHELLO

Well, do it, and be brief. I will walk by.

---

5 monumental i.e., used in making tombs and funeral monuments
7 the light . . . light the torch or lamp . . . Desdemona's life **8 flaming
minister** torch or lamp that serves me **10 repent me** change my
mind **11 Thou . . . pattern** you skillfully wrought perfect example
12 Promethean heat divine fire. (Alluding to the theft of fire from
heaven by Prometheus.) **13 relume** rekindle **21 cruel** unrelenting
22 It . . . love (Compare Hebrews 12:6: "For whom the Lord loveth he
chasteneth.") **28 crime** sin **30 Solicit** petition, pray. **straight**
immediately

I would not kill thy unprepared spirit.
No, heaven forfend! I would not kill thy soul.   34

DESDEMONA
Talk you of killing?

OTHELLO   Ay, I do.

DESDEMONA   Then heaven
Have mercy on me!

OTHELLO   Amen, with all my heart!

DESDEMONA
If you say so, I hope you will not kill me.

OTHELLO   Humh!

DESDEMONA
And yet I fear you; for you're fatal then
When your eyes roll so. Why I should fear I know not,
Since guiltiness I know not; but yet I feel I fear.

OTHELLO
Think on thy sins.

DESDEMONA   They are loves I bear to you.   42

OTHELLO   Ay, and for that thou diest.

DESDEMONA
That death's unnatural that kills for loving.
Alas, why gnaw you so your nether lip?
Some bloody passion shakes your very frame.
These are portents; but yet I hope, I hope,
They do not point on me.   48

OTHELLO   Peace, and be still!

DESDEMONA   I will so. What's the matter?

OTHELLO
That handkerchief which I so loved and gave thee
Thou gav'st to Cassio.

DESDEMONA   No, by my life and soul!
Send for the man and ask him.

OTHELLO
Sweet soul, take heed, take heed of perjury.
Thou art on thy deathbed.

DESDEMONA
Ay, but not yet to die.

OTHELLO   Yes, presently.   56

34 forfend forbid   **42 They are . . . you** i.e., if I sinned, it was in loving you more than my father, or more than God   **48 point on** point at, predict what is to happen to   **56 presently** immediately

Therefore confess thee freely of thy sin;
For to deny each article with oath
Cannot remove nor choke the strong conception   59
That I do groan withal. Thou art to die.   60

DESDEMONA
Then Lord have mercy on me!

OTHELLO   I say, amen.

DESDEMONA
And have you mercy too! I never did
Offend you in my life; never loved Cassio   63
But with such general warranty of heaven   64
As I might love. I never gave him token.

OTHELLO
By heaven, I saw my handkerchief in 's hand.
O perjured woman! Thou dost stone my heart,   67
And makes me call what I intend to do
A murder, which I thought a sacrifice.
I saw the handkerchief.

DESDEMONA   He found it, then.
I never gave it him. Send for him hither;
Let him confess a truth.

OTHELLO   He hath confessed.

DESDEMONA   What, my lord?

OTHELLO
That he hath used thee.

DESDEMONA   How? Unlawfully?

OTHELLO   Ay.

DESDEMONA
He will not say so.

OTHELLO   No, his mouth is stopped;
Honest Iago hath ta'en order for 't.   76

DESDEMONA
O, my fear interprets. What, is he dead?

OTHELLO
Had all his hairs been lives, my great revenge
Had stomach for them all.

DESDEMONA
Alas, he is betrayed and I undone!   [*She weeps.*]

59 conception (1) belief in your guilt (2) plan in my mind   **60 groan
withal** (1) groan at in sorrow (2) groan as in giving birth   **63 Offend**
wrong   **64 warranty** sanction   **67 stone** turn to stone, harden   **76 ta'en
order** taken measures

OTHELLO
  Out, strumpet! Weep'st thou for him to my face?
DESDEMONA
  O, banish me, my lord, but kill me not!
OTHELLO   Down, strumpet!
DESDEMONA
  Kill me tomorrow; let me live tonight!
OTHELLO   Nay, if you strive—
DESDEMONA
  But half an hour!
OTHELLO   Being done, there is no pause.   86
DESDEMONA
  But while I say one prayer!
OTHELLO   It is too late.
                                  Smothers her.

EMILIA (*At the door*)
  My lord, my lord! What ho! My lord, my lord!
OTHELLO
  What noise is this? Not dead? Not yet quite dead?
  I that am cruel am yet merciful;
  I would not have thee linger in thy pain.
                            [*He dispatches her.*]
  So, so.
EMILIA (*Within*)   What ho! My lord, my lord!
OTHELLO   Who's there?
EMILIA [*Within*]

  O, good my lord, I would speak a word with you!
OTHELLO
  Yes, 'tis Emilia.—By and by.—She's dead.
  'Tis like she comes to speak of Cassio's death.—   95
  The noise was here. Ha! No more moving?   96
  Still as the grave. Shall she come in? Were 't good?—
  I think she stirs again. No. What's best to do?
  If she come in, she'll sure speak to my wife.
  My wife! My wife! What wife? I have no wife.
  O, insupportable! O heavy hour!
  Methinks it should be now a huge eclipse

---

86 Being done i.e., since justice has begun its relentless course   **95 like**
likely that   **96 here** (The Folio's *high* is possible, suggesting that the
commotion of the attack on Cassio was loud.)

Of sun and moon, and that th' affrighted globe
Should yawn at alteration.

EMILIA [*Within*]   I do beseech you   104
That I may speak with you, O, good my lord!

OTHELLO
I had forgot thee. O, come in, Emilia.—
Soft, by and by. Let me the curtains draw.—   107
               [*He closes the bed-curtains and
                       opens the door.*]
Where art thou?

    Enter Emilia.

                What's the matter with thee now?

EMILIA
O, my good lord, yonder's foul murders done!

OTHELLO What, now?

EMILIA But now, my lord.

OTHELLO
It is the very error of the moon;   112
She comes more nearer earth than she was wont,
And makes men mad.

EMILIA
Cassio, my lord, hath killed a young Venetian
Called Roderigo.

OTHELLO   Roderigo killed?
And Cassio killed?

EMILIA   No, Cassio is not killed.

OTHELLO
Not Cassio killed? Then murder's out of tune,
And sweet revenge grows harsh.

DESDEMONA O, falsely, falsely murdered!

EMILIA O Lord, what cry is that?

OTHELLO That? What?

EMILIA
Out and alas, that was my lady's voice.   123
              [*She opens the bed-curtains.*]

---

104 yawn gape in amazement, i.e., move in an earthquake. (According to
Pliny, earthquakes often happen during eclipses.) **at alteration** at these
cataclysmic events in nature, well suited to express the horror of Desdemona's death **107 Soft** wait a minute **112 error** aberration, irregular-
ity **123 Out** (A cry of dismay, intensifying *alas*.)

Help, help, ho, help! O lady, speak again!
Sweet Desdemona! O sweet mistress, speak!
DESDEMONA A guiltless death I die.
EMILIA O, who hath done this deed?
DESDEMONA Nobody; I myself. Farewell.
  Commend me to my kind lord. O, farewell! [*She dies.*]
OTHELLO
  Why, how should she be murdered?
EMILIA   Alas, who knows?
OTHELLO
  You heard her say herself it was not I.
EMILIA
  She said so. I must needs report the truth.
OTHELLO
  She's like a liar gone to burning hell!
  'Twas I that killed her.
EMILIA   O, the more angel she,
  And you the blacker devil!
OTHELLO
  She turned to folly, and she was a whore.   136
EMILIA
  Thou dost belie her, and thou art a devil.   137
OTHELLO She was false as water.
EMILIA Thou art rash as fire to say
  That she was false. O, she was heavenly true!
OTHELLO
  Cassio did top her. Ask thy husband else.   141
  O, I were damned beneath all depth in hell
  But that I did proceed upon just grounds
  To this extremity. Thy husband knew it all.
EMILIA My husband?
OTHELLO Thy husband.
EMILIA That she was false to wedlock?
OTHELLO
  Ay, with Cassio. Nay, had she been true,
  If heaven would make me such another world
  Of one entire and perfect chrysolite,   150
  I'd not have sold her for it.
EMILIA My husband?

---

136 folly i.e., wantonness, fleshly sin **137 belie** slander **141 else** i.e., if
you don't believe me **150 chrysolite** precious topaz

OTHELLO
  Ay, 'twas he that told me on her first.
  An honest man he is, and hates the slime
  That sticks on filthy deeds.
EMILIA   My husband?
OTHELLO
  What needs this iterance, woman? I say thy husband.   157
EMILIA
  O mistress, villainy hath made mocks with love!   158
  My husband say she was false?
OTHELLO   He, woman;
  I say thy husband. Dost understand the word?
  My friend, thy husband, honest, honest Iago.
EMILIA
  If he say so, may his pernicious soul
  Rot half a grain a day! He lies to th' heart.
  She was too fond of her most filthy bargain.
OTHELLO   Ha?   [He draws.]
EMILIA   Do thy worst!
  This deed of thine is no more worthy heaven
  Than thou wast worthy her.
OTHELLO   Peace, you were best.   168
EMILIA
  Thou hast not half that power to do me harm
  As I have to be hurt. O gull! O dolt!   170
  As ignorant as dirt! Thou hast done a deed—
  I care not for thy sword; I'll make thee known,
  Though I lost twenty lives.—Help! Help, ho, help!
  The Moor hath killed my mistress! Murder, murder!

        Enter Montano, Gratiano, and Iago.

MONTANO
  What is the matter? How now, General?
EMILIA
  O, are you come, Iago? You have done well,
  That men must lay their murders on your neck.
GRATIANO   What is the matter?
EMILIA [*To Iago*]
  Disprove this villain, if thou be'st a man.

---

157 iterance iteration, repetition   **158 made mocks with** derided, made
sport of   **168 you were best** it would be best for you   **170 to be hurt**
i.e., to endure hurt.   **gull** dupe

He says thou toldst him that his wife was false.
I know thou didst not; thou'rt not such a villain.
Speak, for my heart is full.

IAGO
I told him what I thought, and told no more
Than what he found himself was apt and true.   184

EMILIA
But did you ever tell him she was false?

IAGO   I did.

EMILIA
You told a lie, an odious, damnèd lie!
Upon my soul, a lie, a wicked lie.
She false with Cassio? Did you say with Cassio?

IAGO
With Cassio, mistress. Go to, charm your tongue.   190

EMILIA
I will not charm my tongue; I am bound to speak.
My mistress here lies murdered in her bed—

ALL   O heavens forfend!

EMILIA
And your reports have set the murder on.

OTHELLO
Nay, stare not, masters. It is true indeed.

GRATIANO   'Tis a strange truth.

MONTANO
O monstrous act!

EMILIA   Villainy, villainy, villainy!
I think upon 't—I think I smell 't! O villainy!
I thought so then—I'll kill myself for grief—   199
O villainy, villainy!

IAGO
What, are you mad? I charge you, get you home.

EMILIA
Good gentlemen, let me have leave to speak.
'Tis proper I obey him, but not now.
Perchance, Iago, I will ne'er go home.

184 apt plausible   **190 charm** keep silent (as though by a magic spell)
199 then (Perhaps at 3.3.331–332 and 4.2.137–154.)

OTHELLO
O! O! O!   [*Othello falls on the bed.*]
EMILIA   Nay, lay thee down and roar,   205
For thou hast killed the sweetest innocent
That e'er did lift up eye.
OTHELLO [*Rising*]   O, she was foul!   207
I scarce did know you, uncle. There lies your niece,
Whose breath indeed these hands have newly stopped.
I know this act shows horrible and grim.   210

GRATIANO
Poor Desdemon! I am glad thy father's dead.
Thy match was mortal to him, and pure grief
Shore his old thread in twain. Did he live now,   213
This sight would make him do a desperate turn,   214
Yea, curse his better angel from his side,
And fall to reprobance.   216

OTHELLO
'Tis pitiful. But yet Iago knows
That she with Cassio hath the act of shame
A thousand times committed. Cassio confessed it;
And she did gratify his amorous works   220
With that recognizance and pledge of love   221
Which I first gave her. I saw it in his hand;
It was a handkerchief, an antique token
My father gave my mother.
EMILIA   O God! O heavenly God!

IAGO
Zounds, hold your peace.
EMILIA   'Twill out, 'twill out! I peace?
No, I will speak as liberal as the north.   227
Let heaven and men and devils, let them all,
All, all, cry shame against me, yet I'll speak.

IAGO
Be wise, and get you home.

---

205 s.d. Othello . . . bed (This direction is from the quarto, as also *He kisses her* at l. 19 and *She dies* at l. 129.)   **207 lift up eye** i.e., lift her eyes to heaven   **210 shows** looks   **213 Shore** sheared, cut   **214 turn** deed   **216 reprobance** damnation, i.e., suicide   **220 gratify** reward   **221 recognizance** token   **227 liberal as the north** freely as the north wind (blows)

EMILIA   I will not.
                              [Iago threatens Emilia.]
GRATIANO   Fie,
  Your sword upon a woman?
EMILIA
  O thou dull Moor! That handkerchief thou speak'st of
  I found by fortune and did give my husband;
  For often, with a solemn earnestness,
  More than indeed belonged to such a trifle,   235
  He begged of me to steal 't.
IAGO   Villainous whore!
EMILIA
  She give it Cassio? No, alas! I found it,
  And I did give 't my husband.
IAGO   Filth, thou liest!
EMILIA
  By heaven, I do not, I do not, gentlemen.
  O murderous coxcomb! What should such a fool   240
  Do with so good a wife?
OTHELLO   Are there no stones in heaven   242
  But what serves for the thunder?—Precious villain!   243
              [He runs at Iago; Montano disarms Othello.
                    Iago, from behind, stabs Emilia.]
GRATIANO
  The woman falls! Sure he hath killed his wife.
EMILIA
  Ay, ay. O, lay me by my mistress' side.
                                           [Exit Iago.]
GRATIANO   He's gone, but his wife's killed.
MONTANO
  'Tis a notorious villain. Take you this weapon,
  Which I have here recovered from the Moor.
  Come, guard the door without. Let him not pass,
  But kill him rather. I'll after that same villain,
  For 'tis a damnèd slave.
              Exit [with all but Othello and Emilia,
              who has been laid by Desdemona's side].

235 belonged was appropriate   240 coxcomb fool. (Addressed to
Othello.)   242 stones bolts, such as those used for thunderbolts
243 Precious i.e., arrant, utter   s.d. He . . . Emilia (The quarto text
reads, "The Moor runs at Iago. Iago kills his wife." The quarto also
specifies the exit of Iago at l. 245 and the death of Emilia at l. 260.)

OTHELLO   I am not valiant neither,
But every puny whipster gets my sword.   253
But why should honor outlive honesty?   254
Let it go all.
EMILIA   What did thy song bode, lady?
Hark, canst thou hear me? I will play the swan,
And die in music. [*She sings.*] "Willow, willow, willow."
Moor, she was chaste. She loved thee, cruel Moor.
So come my soul to bliss as I speak true.
So speaking as I think, alas, I die.   [*She dies.*]
OTHELLO
I have another weapon in this chamber;
It was a sword of Spain, the ice-brook's temper—   262
O, here it is. [*He finds a sword.*] Uncle, I must come forth.
GRATIANO [*Within*]
If thou attempt it, it will cost thee dear.
Thou hast no weapon, and perforce must suffer.
OTHELLO
Look in upon me then and speak with me,
Or, naked as I am, I will assault thee.   267

     [*Enter Gratiano.*]

GRATIANO
What is the matter?
OTHELLO   Behold, I have a weapon;
A better never did itself sustain
Upon a soldier's thigh. I have seen the day
That, with this little arm and this good sword,
I have made my way through more impediments
Than twenty times your stop. But O, vain boast!   273
Who can control his fate? 'Tis not so now.
Be not afraid, though you do see me weaponed;
Here is my journey's end, here is my butt   276
And very seamark of my utmost sail.   277
                    [*Gratiano steps back.*]
Do you go back dismayed? 'Tis a lost fear;   278

---

253 whipster contemptible fellow   **254 honor** i.e., the bravery for which
one enjoys a soldier's reputation.   **honesty** true integrity   **262 the ice-
brook's temper** tempered in ice-cold water   **267 naked** unarmed
273 stop power (to stop)   **276 butt** goal, limit. (An archery term.)
277 seamark beacon (marking his destination or limit)   **278 lost** wasted,
unneeded

Man but a rush against Othello's breast   279
And he retires. Where should Othello go?
        [*He turns to Desdemona.*]
Now, how dost thou look now? O ill-starred wench!
Pale as thy smock! When we shall meet at compt,   282
This look of thine will hurl my soul from heaven,
And fiends will snatch at it. Cold, cold, my girl?
Even like thy chastity. O cursèd, cursèd slave!   285
Whip me, ye devils,
From the possession of this heavenly sight!
Blow me about in winds! Roast me in sulfur!
Wash me in steep-down gulfs of liquid fire!
O Desdemon! Dead, Desdemon! Dead! O! O!   290

    Enter Lodovico, Cassio [carried in a litter],
    Montano, and Iago [prisoner], with officers.

LODOVICO
Where is this rash and most unfortunate man?
OTHELLO
That's he that was Othello. Here I am.
LODOVICO
Where is that viper? Bring the villain forth.
        [*Iago is led forward.*]
OTHELLO
I look down towards his feet; but that's a fable.   294
If that thou be'st a devil, I cannot kill thee.
        [*He wounds Iago.*]
LODOVICO
Wrench his sword from him.   [*Othello is disarmed.*]
IAGO   I bleed, sir, but not killed.
OTHELLO
I am not sorry neither. I'd have thee live,
For in my sense 'tis happiness to die.   298
LODOVICO
O thou Othello, that was once so good,
Fall'n in the practice of a cursèd slave,   300
What shall be said to thee?

---

279 Man . . . rush wield no more than a reed   **282 compt** account,
judgment day   **285 slave** i.e., Othello himself   **290 s.d. in a litter** (The
quarto specifies that Cassio is "in a chair.")   **294 towards his feet** i.e.,
to see if they are cloven like the devil's   **298 in my sense** to one who
feel as I do   **300 in the practice** through the plotting. **slave** villain

OTHELLO   Why, anything.
An honorable murderer, if you will,
For naught I did in hate, but all in honor.

LODOVICO
This wretch hath part confessed his villainy.
Did you and he consent in Cassio's death?   305

OTHELLO   Ay.

CASSIO
Dear General, I never gave you cause.

OTHELLO
I do believe it, and I ask your pardon.
Will you, I pray, demand that demi-devil
Why he hath thus ensnared my soul and body?

IAGO
Demand me nothing. What you know, you know.
From this time forth I never will speak word.

LODOVICO   What, not to pray?

GRATIANO   Torments will ope your lips.   314

OTHELLO   Well, thou dost best.

LODOVICO
Sir, you shall understand what hath befall'n,
Which, as I think, you know not. Here is a letter
Found in the pocket of the slain Roderigo;
And here another. [*He produces letters.*] The one of them
   imports
The death of Cassio, to be undertook
By Roderigo.

OTHELLO
O villain!

CASSIO   Most heathenish and most gross!   322

LODOVICO [*Showing another paper*]
Now here's another discontented paper   323
Found in his pocket too. And this, it seems,
Roderigo meant t' have sent this damnèd villain;
But that belike Iago in the interim   326
Came in and satisfied him.   327

OTHELLO   O thou pernicious caitiff!—
How came you, Cassio, by that handkerchief
That was my wife's?

305 consent agree   **314 Torments** torture   **322 gross** monstrous   **323 discontented** full of discontent   **326 belike** most likely   **327 Came in**
interposed

CASSIO   I found it in my chamber;
   And he himself confessed it but even now
   That there he dropped it for a special purpose
   Which wrought to his desire.
OTHELLO   O fool, fool, fool!   333
CASSIO
   There is besides in Roderigo's letter
   How he upbraids Iago, that he made him
   Brave me upon the watch, whereon it came   336
   That I was cast; and even but now he spake,   337
   After long seeming dead, Iago hurt him,
   Iago set him on.
LODOVICO [*To Othello*]
   You must forsake this room and go with us.
   Your power and your command is taken off,   341
   And Cassio rules in Cyprus. For this slave,
   If there be any cunning cruelty
   That can torment him much and hold him long,   344
   It shall be his. You shall close prisoner rest   345
   Till that the nature of your fault be known
   To the Venetian state.—Come, bring away.
OTHELLO
   Soft you; a word or two before you go.   348
   I have done the state some service, and they know 't.
   No more of that. I pray you, in your letters,
   When you shall these unlucky deeds relate,   351
   Speak of me as I am; nothing extenuate,
   Nor set down aught in malice. Then must you speak
   Of one that loved not wisely but too well;
   Of one not easily jealous but, being wrought,   355
   Perplexed in the extreme; of one whose hand,   356
   Like the base Indian, threw a pearl away   357

---

333 wrought . . . desire worked out as he wished, fitted in with his
plan   **336 Brave** defy   **337 cast** dismissed   **341 taken off** taken away
344 hold him long keep him alive a long time (during his torture)
345 rest remain   **348 Soft you** one moment   **351 unlucky** unfortunate
355 wrought worked upon   **356 Perplexed** distraught   **357 Indian** (This
reading from the quarto pictures an ignorant savage who cannot recognize the value of a precious jewel. The Folio reading, *Iudean* or *Judean*,
i.e., infidel or disbeliever, may refer to Herod, who slew Miriamne in a
fit of jealousy, or to Judas Iscariot, the betrayer of Christ.)

Richer than all his tribe; of one whose subdued eyes,   358
Albeit unusèd to the melting mood,
Drops tears as fast as the Arabian trees
Their medicinable gum. Set you down this;   361
And say besides that in Aleppo once,
Where a malignant and a turbaned Turk
Beat a Venetian and traduced the state,
I took by th' throat the circumcisèd dog
And smote him, thus.   [*He stabs himself.*]   366
LODOVICO   O bloody period!   367
GRATIANO   All that is spoke is marred.
OTHELLO
I kissed thee ere I killed thee. No way but this,
Killing myself, to die upon a kiss.
                    [*He kisses Desdemona and*] *dies.*

CASSIO
This did I fear, but thought he had no weapon;
For he was great of heart.
LODOVICO [*To Iago*]   O Spartan dog,   372
More fell than anguish, hunger, or the sea!   373
Look on the tragic loading of this bed.
This is thy work. The object poisons sight;
Let it be hid. Gratiano, keep the house,   376
                    [*The bed-curtains are drawn*]
And seize upon the fortunes of the Moor,   377
For they succeed on you. [*To Cassio.*] To you, Lord
    Governor,   378
Remains the censure of this hellish villain,   379
The time, the place, the torture. O, enforce it!
Myself will straight aboard, and to the state
This heavy act with heavy heart relate.   *Exeunt.*

---

358 subdued i.e., overcome by grief   **361 gum** i.e., myrrh   **366 s.d. He stabs himself** (This direction is in the quarto text.)   **367 period** termination, conclusion   **372 Spartan dog** (Spartan dogs were noted for their savagery and silence.)   **373 fell** cruel   **376 Let it be hid** i.e., draw the bed-curtains. (No stage direction specifies that the dead are to be carried offstage at the end of the play.)   **keep** remain in   **377 seize upon** take legal possession of   **378 succeed on** pass as though by inheritance to   **379 censure** sentencing

Date and Text

On October 6, 1621, Thomas Walkley entered in the Stationers' Register, the official record book of the London Company of Stationers (booksellers and printers), "The Tragedie of Othello, the moore of Venice," and published the play in the following year:

> THE Tragoedy of Othello, The Moore of Venice. *As it hath beene diuerse times acted at the* Globe, and at the Black-Friers, by *his Maiesties Seruants. Written by* VVilliam Shakespeare. *LONDON*, Printed by *N. O.* [Nicholas Okes] for *Thomas Walkley*, and are to be sold at his shop, at the Eagle and Child, in Brittans Bursse. 1622.

The text of this quarto is a good one, based probably on a transcript of Shakespeare's foul papers (working manuscript), although it is some 160 lines shorter than the Folio text of 1623 and may have been cut in the printing house to meet the constraints of space when the printer's copy was allocated to a fixed number of pages. The Folio text may have been derived (via an intermediate transcript) from a copy of the original foul papers, one in which Shakespeare himself copied over his work and made a large number of synonymous or nearly synonymous changes as he did so. These papers, edited by someone else to remove profanity as required by law and introducing other stylistic changes in the process, seemingly became the basis of the promptbook and also of the Folio text.

The textual situation is thus complex. The Folio text appears to contain a significant number of authorial changes, but it was also worked on by one or more sophisticated scribes and by compositors whose changes are sometimes hard to distinguish from those of Shakespeare. The quarto text was printed by a printing establishment not known for careful work, but does stand close in some ways to a Shakespearean original. Editorially, then, the Folio's readings are to be preferred when the quarto is not clearly right and especially when the Folio gives us genuinely new words; but the quarto's readings demand careful consideration when the Folio text may be suspected of mechanical error (e.g., the shortening of words in full lines) or compositorial substitution of alternative forms, normalizations, and easy adjustments of meter. There are times when the Folio's compositor may have been misled by nearby words or letters in his copy. And because the Folio's stage directions are probably scribal, attention should be paid to those in the quarto.

The earliest mention of the play is on "Hallamas Day, being the first of Nouembar," 1604, when "the Kings Maiesties plaiers" performed "A Play in the Banketinge house att Whit Hall Called The Moor of Venis." The play is attributed to "Shaxberd." The authenticity of this Revels account, first printed by Peter Cunningham in 1842, was once challenged, but it is now accepted as genuine. On stylistic grounds the play is usually dated in 1603 or 1604, although arguments are sometimes presented for a date as early as 1601 or 1602.

Textual Notes

These textual notes are not a historical collation, either of the early quartos and folios or of more recent editions; they are simply a record of departures in this edition from the copy text. The reading adopted in this edition appears in boldface, followed by the rejected reading from the copy text, i.e., the First Folio. Only major alterations in punctuation are noted. Changes in lineation are not indicated, nor are some minor and obvious typographical errors.

Abbreviations used:
F the First Folio
Q1 the quarto of 1622
s.d. stage direction
s.p. speech prefix

Copy text: the First Folio. The adopted readings are from the quarto of 1622 [Q1], unless otherwise indicated; [eds.] means that the adopted reading was first proposed by some editor subsequent to the First Folio.

1.1. 1 Tush, never Neuer   **4 'Sblood, but** but   **16 And, in conclusion** [Q1; not in F]   **26 togaed** Tongued   **30 other** others   **34 God bless** blesse   **68 full** fall   **thick-lips** Thick-lips   **74 changes** chances   **75 [and elsewhere] lose** [eds.] loose   **81 Thieves, thieves, thieves** Theeues, Theeues   **83 s.d. Brabantio above** [in F, printed as a speech prefix to l. 84]   **88 Zounds, sir** Sir [also at l. 111]   **103 bravery** knauerie   **119 are now** are   **158 pains** apines   **161 sign. That** [eds.] signe) that   **186 night** might

1.2. 15 and or   **34 Duke** Dukes   **50 carrack** Carract   **64 her!** [eds.] her   **69 darlings** Dearelng   **89 I do** do

1.3. 1 There is There's   **these** this   **61 s.p. Duke and Senators** [All Q1] Sen   **101 maimed** main'd   **108 s.p. Duke** [Q1; not in F]   **109 overt** ouer   **112 s.p. [and elsewhere] First Senator** Sen   **124 till** tell   **132 battles** Battaile   **fortunes** Fortune   **141 travels'** Trauellours   **143 rocks, and** Rocks   **heads** head   **145 other** others   **147 Do grow** Grew   **149 thence** hence   **157 intentively** instinctiuely   **161 sighs** kisses   **204 Into your favor** [Q1; not in F]   **222 ear** eares   **227 sovereign** more soueraigne   **233 couch** [eds.] Coach [F] Cooch [Q1]   **237 These** [eds.] This   **244 Nor I. I would not** Nor would I   **251 did love** loue   **267 me** [eds.] my   **273 instruments** Instrument   **281 Desdemona. Tonight, my lord? Duke. This night** [Q1; not in F]   **285 With** And   **294 s.p. First Senator** Sen   **296 s.d. Exeunt** Exit   **302 matters** matter   **303 the** the the   **329 beam** [eds.] braine [F] ballance [Q1]   **333–334 our unbitted** or vnbitted   **335 scion** [eds.] Seyen [F] syen [Q1]   **353 error** errors   **354 She . . . she must** [Q1; not in F]   **358 a supersubtle** super-subtle   **378–382 Roderigo. What . . . purse** [Q1; not in F]   **386 a snipe** Snpe   **389 He's** [Ha's Q1] She ha's   **396 ear** eares

2.1. 35 prays praye   **36 heaven** Heauens   **42 s.p. Third Gentleman** Gent   **44 arrivance** Arriuancie   **45 this** the   **58 s.p. Second Gentleman** Gent [also at ll. 61, 68, and 95]   **72 clog** enclogge   **84 And . . . comfort** [Q1; not in F]   **90 tell me** tell   **94 the sea** Sea   **96 their** this   **107 list** leaue   **111 doors**

doore **156 [and elsewhere] ne'er** neu'r   **158 such wight** such wightes
170 gyve [eds.] giue   **174 An** and   **175 courtesy** Curtsie   **176 clyster pipes**
Cluster-pipes   **214 s.d. Exeunt** [eds.] Exit   **216 hither** thither   **229 again** a
game   **239 fortune** Forune   **242 compassing** compasse   **244 finder out**
finder   **occasions** occasion   **has** he's   **263 mutualities** mutabilities
300 for wife for wift   **307 rank** right   **308 nightcap** Night-Cape

2.2. 6 addiction [eds.] addition   **10 Heaven bless** Blesse

2.3. 27 stoup [eds.] stope   **38 unfortunate** infortunate   **52 lads** else   **57 to**
put to   **61, 71 God** heauen   **76 Englishman** Englishmen   **91 Then . . .**
auld [Then . . . owd *Q1*] And take thy awl'd   **93 'Fore God** Why   **97 God's**
heau'ns   **106 God forgive** Forgiue   **110 speak** I speake   **123 the** his
138 s.d. Cry within: Help! Help [from Q1: "Helpe, helpe, within"]
139 Zounds, you You   **152 God's will** Alas   **153 Montano—sir** Montano
156 God's will, Lieutenant, hold Fie, fie Lieutenant   **158 Zounds, I** I
161 sense of place [eds.] place of sense   **177 breast** breastes   **184 wont be**
wont to be   **201 Zounds, if I** If I once   **212 leagued** [eds.] league   **218 Thus**
This   **227 the** then   **246 well now** well   **250 vile** vil'd   **255 God** Heauen
260 thought had thought   **266 ways** more wayes   **283 O God** Oh   **308 I'll**
.   **311 denotement** [eds.] deuotement   **325–326 me here** me   **337 were 't**
were   **369 hast** hath   **372 By the Mass** Introth   **378 on;** [on, *Q1*] on   **379 the**
[eds.] a

3.1. s.d. Musicians [eds.] Musicians, and Clowne   **21 s.d. Exeunt** [eds.]
Exit   **22 hear** heare me   **26 General's wife** Generall   **31 Cassio. Do, good**
my friend [Q1, not in F]   **42 s.d. Exit** [at l. 41 in F]   **52 To . . . front** [Q1; not
in F]

3.3. 16 circumstance Circumstances   **41 you** your   **55 Yes, faith** I sooth
56 or on   **80 By'r Lady** Trust me   **103 you** he   **118 By heaven** Alas   **124 In**
Of   **148 that all** that: All   **free to** free   **152 But some** Wherein   **160 oft** of
161 wisdom then wisdome   **175 By heaven, I'll** Ile   **183 fondly** [eds.]
soundly [F] strongly [Q1]   **188 God** Heauen   **194 Is once** Is   **196 blown**
blow'd   **199 dances well** Dances   **216 God** Heauen   **218 keep 't** [eds.] keepe
[Q1] kept [F]   **230 I' faith** Trust me   **232 my** your   **249 disproportion**
disproportions   **264 to hold** to   **275 qualities** Quantities   **289 of** to   **294 O,**
then heaven mocks** Heauen mock'd   **301 Faith** Why   **305 s.d. Exit** [at l. 304
in F]   **328 faith** but   **345 s.d. Enter Othello** [after "I did say so" in F]
354 of her in her   **385 remorse;** [remorce. *Q1*] remorse   **407 see, sir** see
411 supervisor super-vision   **439 then laid** laid   **440 Over** ore   **sighed**
sigh   **kissed** kisse   **441 Cried** cry   **455 any that was** [eds.] any, it was
468 mind perhaps minde   **471 Ne'er feels** [eds.] Neu'r keepes

3.4. 23 that the   **37 It yet** It   **56 faith** indeed   **77 I' faith** Indeed   **79 God**
Heauen   **83 Heaven bless** Blesse   **88 can, sir** can   **94–95 Desdemona. I pray**
. . Cassio. Othello. The handkerchief! [Q1; not in F]   **99 I' faith** Insooth
100 Zounds Away   **164 that** the   **172 I' faith** Indeed   **182 friend.** [eds.]
friend,   **183 absence** [eds.] absence, [Q1] Absence: [F]   **188 by my faith** in
good troth

4.1. 32 Faith Why   **36 Zounds, that's** that's   **45 work** workes   **52 No,**
forbear [Q1; not in F]   **72 couch** [Coach *Q1*] Cowch;   **79 unsuiting** [Q1
corrected] vnfitting [Q1 uncorrected] resulting [F]   **97 clothes** Cloath
103 conster conserue   **105 you now** you   **109 power** dowre   **114 i' faith**

indeed   **121 Do you** Do ye   **122 marry her** marry   **125 win** [eds.] winnes
126 Faith Why   **shall marry** marry   **133 beckons** becomes   **137 by this
hand, she** [Q1; not in F]   **163 Faith, I** I   **165 Faith** Yes   **212 s.d.** [at. l. 210 in
F]   **215 God save** Saue   **238 By my troth** Trust me   **251 Truly, an** Truely
284 denote deonte [F uncorrected] deuote [F corrected]

4.2. 32 Nay May   **33 knees** knee   **35 But not the words** [Q1; not in F]
51 kinds kind   **56 A** The   **66 Ay, there** [eds.] I heere   **71 ne'er** neuer
83 Impudent strumpet [Q1; not in F]   **96 keep** [eds.] keepes   **s.d. Enter
Emilia** [at l. 94 in F]   **162 them in** [eds.] them: or   **174 And . . . you** [Q1; not
in F]   **177 you to** to   **190 Faith, I** I   **for** and   **201 By this hand** Nay
232 takes taketh   **236 of** [Q1; not in F]

4.3. 10 s.d. Exit [at l. 9 in F]   **22 favor in them** fauour   **25 faith** Father
26 before thee before   **43 sighing** [eds.] singing [F corrected] sining [F
uncorrected]   **73 Good troth** Introth   **74 By my troth** Introth   **78 Uds pity
why**   **107 God** Heauen

5.1. 1 bulk Barke   **22 Be 't But**   **hear** heard   **36 Forth** For   **50 Did** Do
91 O heaven Yes, 'tis   **106 out o'** o'   **113 'Las, what's . . . What's** Alas, what
is . . . What is   **116 dead** quite dead   **126 Faugh! Fie** Fie

5.2. 34 heaven Heauens   **37 say so** say   **56 Yes, presently** Presently
61 Then Lord O Heauen   **96 here** high   **104 Should** Did   **121 O Lord** Alas
131 heard heare   **148 Nay, had** had   **225 O God! O heavenly God** Oh
Heauen! oh heauenly Powres   **226 Zounds** Come   **248 have here** haue
317 not. Here [not: here *Q1*] not) heere   **357 Indian** Iudean

Shakespeare's Sources

Shakespeare's main source for *Othello* was the seventh story from the third decade of G. B. Giraldi Cinthio's *Hecatommithi* (1565). Cinthio was available in French but not in English translation during Shakespeare's lifetime. The verbal echoes in Shakespeare's play are usually closer to the Italian original than to Gabriel Chappuys's French version of 1584. Cinthio's account may have been based on an actual incident occurring in Venice around 1508.

Shakespeare is considerably indebted to Cinthio's story for the essentials of the narrative, as can be seen in the following new translation: the marriage of a Moorish captain to a Venetian lady, Disdemona, whose relatives wish her to marry someone else, the mutual attraction to noble qualities of mind in both husband and wife, their happiness together at first, the dispatching of the Moor to Cyprus to take charge of the garrison there, Disdemona's insistence on accompanying her husband through whatever dangers may occur (though the sea voyage, as it turns out, is a very calm one), the ensign's treachery and resolve to destroy the Moor's happiness with Disdemona, her begging her husband to reinstate the squadron leader whom the Moor has demoted for fighting on guard duty (although no mention is made of drunkenness or of the ensign's role in starting the trouble), the ensign's insinuations to the Moor that his wife is cuckolding him because she is becoming weary of her marriage with a black man, the ensign's difficulty in providing ocular proof, his planting of Disdemona's handkerchief in the squadron leader's quarters and his showing the Moor that the handkerchief is now in the squadron leader's possession, his arranging for the Moor to witness at a distance a conversation between the ensign and squadron leader that is in fact not about Disdemona, Disdemona's confusion when she is asked to produce the handkerchief, the attack on the squadron leader in the dark, the murder of Disdemona in her bed, the Moor's deep regret at the loss of his wife, the eventual punishment of both the Moor and the ensign, and the telling of the story publicly by the ensign's wife, who has heretofore kept silent because of her fear of her husband.

Although these correspondences in the story are many, Shakespeare has changed a great deal. He provides Desdemona with a caring and saddened father, Brabantio, out of Cinthio's brief suggestion of family opposition to her marriage, and adds the entire opening scene in which Iago arouses the prejudices of Brabantio. Roderigo is a brilliantly invented character used to reveal Iago's skill in manipulation. Cinthio's ensign, though thoroughly wicked, never expresses a resentment for the squadron leader's promotion and favored treatment by the Moor; instead, the ensign lusts for Disdemona and turns against her and the Moor only when his passion is unrequited. In his complex portrayal of a consuming and irrational jealousy in Iago, Shakespeare goes far beyond his source, making use as well of the inventive villainy of the Vice in the English late medieval morality play. In Cinthio's account the ensign filches the handkerchief from Disdemona while she is hugging the ensign's three-year-old daughter; the ensign's wife is uninvolved in this mischief, though she does unwillingly learn of her husband's villainy (since he has an idea of using her in his plot) and later feels constrained to hold her tongue when Disdemona asks her if she knows why the Moor is behaving so strangely. (As is usual in prose narrative, the passage of time is much more extended than in Shakespeare's play.)

In the later portions of the story, the changes are more marked. Cinthio relates an episode in which the squadron leader, finding the handkerchief in his room, takes it back to Disdemona while the Moor is out but is interrupted by the Moor's unexpected return home; Shakespeare instead has Cassio approach Desdemona (earlier in the story) to beg her assistance in persuading Othello to reinstate him. Cinthio tells of a woman in the squadron leader's household who copies the embroidery of the handkerchief before it is returned and is seen with it at a window by the Moor; here Shakespeare finds a suggestion for Bianca, but her role is considerably augmented, partly with the help of a passing remark in Cinthio that the squadron leader is attacked and wounded as he leaves the house of a courtesan with whom he occasionally takes his pleasure. In the absence of any haracter corresponding to Roderigo, the Cinthio narrative ssigns to the ensign himself the role of wounding the quadron leader. The manner in which Disdemona is murered is strikingly different. Cinthio has nothing equivalent ɔ the tender scene between Desdemona and Emilia as csdemona prepares to go to bed. Cinthio's Moor hides the nsign in a dressing room next to his bedroom and commisions the ensign to bludgeon her to death with a sand-filled tocking, after which the two murderers cause the ceiling f the room to collapse on her and create the impression hat a rafter has smashed her skull.

Cinthio also treats the aftermath of the murder in a very ifferent way. The Moor, distracted with grief, turns on the nsign and demotes him, whereupon the ensign persuades he squadron commander to take vengeance on the Moor as is attacker (according to the lying ensign) and killer of Disemona. When the squadron commander accuses the Moor efore the Seigniory, the Moor keeps silent but is banished nd eventually killed by Disdemona's relatives. The ensign, eturning to his own country, gets in trouble by making a alse accusation and dies as the result of torture. Cinthio ees this as God's retribution. The ensign's wife lives to tell er story, unlike Shakespeare's Emilia.

The changed ending is essential to Shakespeare's play. milia becomes a more complex figure than the ensign's ife: Shakespeare implicates her in the taking of the handerchief but also accentuates her love for Desdemona and er brave denunciation of her husband when at last she nows the full truth. Othello's ritual slaying of Desdemona voids the appalling butchery of the source story. Shakepeare's ending is more unified, and brings both Othello nd Iago to account for the deeds they have committed in nis play. Most important, Shakespeare transforms a sensaonal murder story into a moving tragedy of love.

Hecatommithi (A Hundred Tales)
By Giovanni Battista Giraldi Cinthio
Translated by David Bevington and Kate Bevington

THIRD DECADE, SEVENTH NOVELLA

*A Moorish captain takes as his wife a woman who is a citi
zen of Venice. An ensign in his company accuses her to he
husband of adultery. The husband undertakes to have th
ensign kill the supposed adulterer. The captain kills hi
wife. Having been publicly accused by the ensign, the Moo
does not confess but is banished nonetheless on clear ev
dence of guilt. The villainous ensign, thinking to harm sti
other persons, brings on himself a wretched death.*

There once lived in Venice a Moor, a very brave man, who
by virtue of his personal qualities and by having given proo
in war of great prudence and energetic ability, was highl
regarded by those signors who, in rewarding honorabl
actions, ever advance the interests of the republic. Now i
happened that a virtuous lady of marvelous beauty, calle
Disdemona, drawn not by a woman's appetite but the in
nate qualities of the Moor himself, fell in love with him. An
he, vanquished by her beauty and nobleness of mind, simi
larly burned with love for the lady. Their love was so well
disposed and mutual that, although the lady's relatives di
what they could to get her to choose some other husband
the two were united in matrimony. And they lived togethe
in such peace and harmony, while they were in Venice, tha
nothing but affectionate words ever passed between them
Now it happened that the signors of Venice made
change in the garrison they maintained on Cyprus, and the
chose the Moor to command the troops they dispatche
there. He, although greatly pleased by the honor thus of
fered him—since such a distinguished rank is conferre
only on men who are noble, mighty, and loyal, and who hav
shown themselves to be unusually brave—was not so happ
when he considered the length and dangers of the voyage
thinking that Disdemona would be distressed by it. But th
lady, who had no other happiness on earth than the Moo

and was greatly pleased with the testimonial to his merits that her husband had received from so powerful and noble a republic, eagerly awaited the hour when her husband, with his men, should set forth on his way, and she accompanying him to such an honorable post.

It grieved her to see the Moor troubled. And so, not knowing what the reason could be, she said to him one day as they sat at dinner: "Why is it, my Moor, that you, who have been promoted to such a distinguished rank by the Seigniory, are nevertheless so depressed?"

The Moor said to Disdemona: "The love I have for you troubles my contentedness with the honor I have received, because I see that one of two things must necessarily happen: either I must take you with me over the perils of the sea, or I must leave you in Venice to avoid this hardship. The first of these cannot help but weigh heavily on me, since every fatigue you endured and every danger we encountered would make me extremely anxious. The second of these, having to leave you behind, would be hateful to me, since in parting from you I should be parting from my very life."

Disdemona, hearing this, said: "Alas, my husband, what thoughts are these that are going through your head? Why do you give in to such vexing ideas? I want to come with you wherever you go, even if I should have to walk through fire in my chemise rather than going by sea in a perfectly safe and handsomely furnished ship. If there are going to be dangers and fatigues, I want to share them with you. I would think you didn't love me very much if you thought of leaving me in Venice rather than taking me to sea with you, or persuaded yourself that I would prefer to stay here in safety rather than be with you in such danger. I want you to get ready for the voyage with all the cheerfulness your seniority of rank deserves."

The Moor threw his arms joyfully around his wife's neck and said with an affectionate kiss: "May God keep us long in such love, my dear wife!"

Soon after that, putting on his armor and making everything ready for the expedition, he went on board the galley with his lady and all their followers, hoisted sail, and got under way, and, favored with a perfectly tranquil sea, they made their journey to Cyprus.

Among the officers of the Moor's company was an ensign, a man of handsome appearance but of the most depraved nature in the world. He was much in favor with the Moor who didn't have the slightest idea of his wickedness. For although his mind was utterly vile, he concealed that villainy in his heart with such high-sounding and noble speech and such pleasing demeanor that he made himself out to be a veritable Hector or Achilles. This rascal had also taken his wife, a beautiful and virtuous young woman, to Cyprus, and being of Italian birth, she was much loved by the Moor's wife, who spent the greater part of the day with her.

In the same company there was also a squadron leader of whom the Moor was very fond. He went often to the Moor's house and frequently dined with him and his wife. And so the lady, knowing how much he meant to her husband, gave him proofs of the greatest kindness. This greatly pleased the Moor.

The villainous ensign, not heeding at all the vows he had made to his wife or the friendship, loyalty, and duty he owed the Moor, fell head over heels in love with Disdemona and bent all his thoughts to see if he could enjoy her, but he didn't dare show his passion openly for fear that, if the Moor should notice, he would quickly be a dead man. And so he sought various ways, as guilefully as he could, to let the lady know that he loved her. But she, who was so entirely taken up with the Moor, never gave a thought to the ensign or anyone else. Everything he did to kindle passion in her toward him had no more effect than as if he hadn't even tried.

Then he took it into his head that this neglect was the result of her being in love with the squadron leader, and he began to wonder how he might remove this person from her sight. Not only did his mind turn to this, but the love he had for the lady changed into the bitterest hatred, and he gave himself entirely to the study of how he might bring it about that, once the squadron leader had been killed, if he himself could not enjoy the lady, the Moor would not be able to enjoy her either.

Turning over in his mind various ideas, all of them villainous and evil, the ensign finally decided to accuse her of adultery to her husband and to make him believe that the adulterer was none other than the squadron leader. But, knowing the single-hearted love the Moor had for Disdemona, and the friendship he had for the squadron leader, the ensign recognized clearly that, unless he could dupe the Moor with some clever fraud, it would be impossible to get him to listen to either accusation. For which reason he set himself to wait until time and place should open up a way for him to begin his villainous project.

Not long afterward, it happened that the Moor, because the squadron leader drew his sword on a soldier while on guard duty and wounded him, demoted him in rank. This distressed Disdemona greatly. Many times she tried to bring about a reconciliation between her husband and him. At this the Moor said to the villainous ensign that his wife was putting up such a fuss on behalf of the squadron leader that he feared he would be constrained at last to reinstate the officer. The villain took this opportunity to set in motion the deception he had planned, and said: "Perhaps Disdemona has good reason to look so kindly on him."

"And why would that be?" said the Moor.

"I have no desire," answered the ensign, "to come between husband and wife, but if you keep your eyes open, you'll see for yourself."

Nothing the Moor did could persuade the ensign to go beyond what he had said. Nevertheless, his words left such a sharp, stinging thorn in the Moor's mind that he gave himself up to thinking intently what these words could mean, and he fell into a deep melancholy.

One day, when his wife was trying to soften his anger toward the squadron leader, beseeching him not to consign to oblivion the service and friendship of so many years for a mere peccadillo, especially since matters had been patched up between the squadron leader and the soldier he wounded, the Moor burst into a rage and said to her: "There must be some extraordinary reason, Disdemona, that you should take so much trouble over this man. He isn't your brother, after all, or even a kinsman, to be so near your heart."

The lady said, courteously and humbly: "Please don't be angry with me. Nothing prompts me to do this except that it saddens me to see you deprived of such a dear friend as I

know, by your own testimony, the squadron leader has been
to you. He hasn't done anything to deserve so much hatred
from you. But you Moors are so naturally hot-tempered that
every little thing provokes you to anger and revenge."

The Moor, made still angrier by these words, answered
"Anyone who doesn't believe this can easily find proof that
it's true! I will be revenged for the wrongs done to me! I will
be satisfied!"

The lady was frightened at these words, and, seeing her
husband to be inflamed with anger against her, quite beyond his usual self, she said humbly: "I have only the best
of motives in speaking to you about this. But, not to give you
any cause to be angry with me, I won't say another word
about it from now on."

Seeing the earnestness with which his wife had pleaded
anew on behalf of the squadron leader, the Moor guessed
that the words which the ensign had spoken to him signi-
fied that Disdemona was in love with the squadron leader.
And so, deeply depressed, he went to the villainous ensign
and tried to get him to speak more frankly. The ensign, bent
on doing injury to the unfortunate lady, after pretending
not to want to say anything that might displease the Moor
gave the appearance of being brought around by the Moor's
urging and said: "I can't deny that it pains me terribly to
have to say anything to you that must disturb you extremely. But since you insist I tell you, and since the concern I ought to have for your honor as my commanding
officer also spurs me on to tell you, I will not now refuse to
obey your request and my own sense of duty. You must realize, then, that your lady's only reason for being unhappy to
see the squadron leader out of favor with you is that she
takes her pleasure with him whenever he comes to your
house. That's how she consoles herself for the disgust she
feels about your blackness."

These words penetrated to the very core of the Moor's
heart. But, in order to know more (though he now believed
what the ensign had told him to be true, through the suspicion that had already been born in his mind), he said, with a
fierce expression: "I don't know what keeps me from cutting
out that audacious tongue of yours, which has had the ef-
frontery to offer such an insult to my lady."

Then the ensign said: "I didn't expect, Captain, any other reward for my friendly service. But, since the duty I owe you and the care I have for your honor have brought me thus far, let me repeat to you that matters stand just as you've heard. And if your lady, with her show of affection for you, has blinded your eyes to such an extent that you are unable to see what is right in front of you, that doesn't at all mean that I haven't been telling the truth. Believe me, this same squadron leader, being one of those people who don't think their happiness complete until they have made some-one else acquainted with it, has told me everything." And he added: "If I hadn't feared your anger, I should, when he told me this, have given him the recompense he justly de-served by killing him. But since, by letting you know what concerns you more than any other person, I have earned for myself such an unbefitting reward, I wish I had kept silent and thus avoided falling into your disfavor."

Then the Moor, in torment, said: "If you do not make me see with my own eyes what you've told me, rest assured that I will give you reason to think you would have been better off to have been born without a tongue."

"It would have been easy enough," answered the scoun-drel, "when he used to come to your house. But now that you have driven him away—and, I must say, not for any compelling need but for the most trivial of reasons—it's bound to be difficult for me, for, even though I feel sure that he enjoys Disdemona whenever you give him the chance, he must do so much more cautiously than before, now that he sees he has fallen into your disfavor. Still, I do not lose hope of being able to make you see what you are so unwilling to believe." And with these words they went their own ways.

The wretched Moor, as if struck by the most piercing of arrows, went home to await the day when the ensign would make him see that which would make him forever unhappy. But the ensign meanwhile was no less troubled by the chaste behavior with which he knew the lady to govern her-self, since it seemed to him impossible to discover a way of making the Moor believe what he had falsely told him. And so, turning this over in his mind in every possible direction, the scoundrel hit at last on a new piece of cunning.

As I have told you, the Moor's wife often went to the house

of the ensign's wife and spent the better part of the day with her. Whereupon the ensign, seeing that she sometimes carried with her a handkerchief which, he knew, the Moor had given her, and which had been embroidered with an intricate Moorish design, and which was especially dear to the lady and no less so to the Moor, he devised a scheme to take it from her by stealth and thereby prepare her final ruin. He had a young daughter, three years old, and much beloved of Disdemona. One day, when the poor lady had gone to pass the time of day at the villain's house, he took up the little girl in his arms and presented her to the lady, who took the child and hugged her to her breast. The traitor, who was very quick in sleight of hand, lifted the handkerchief from her sash so adroitly that she took no notice. And so, glad at heart, he took his leave of her.

Disdemona, unaware of what had happened, went home and, busy with other considerations, never gave a thought to the handkerchief. But a few days afterward, when she went to look for it and couldn't find it, she was terribly afraid that the Moor would ask her for it as he often did.

Meantime the villainous ensign, taking a suitable occasion, visited the squadron leader in his room and, with crafty malice, left the handkerchief at the head of the bed in such a way that the squadron leader took no notice until the following morning when, as he got out of bed, and the handkerchief by this time having fallen to the floor, he put his foot on it. Not being able to imagine how it had gotten into his house, knowing it to be Disdemona's, he determined to give it back to her. And so, waiting until the Moor had gone out, he went to the back door and knocked.

Fortune seemed to have conspired with the ensign to bring about the death of the poor woman, for at that very moment the Moor came back home. Hearing a knock at the door, he went to a window and very angrily shouted: "Who is knocking?" The squadron leader, hearing the Moor' voice and fearing that he would come downstairs and do him some harm, without answering a word took to his heels. The Moor ran downstairs and, opening the door, went out into the street and looked around but found no one. Then, going back inside, filled with spite, he demanded of his wife who it was that had knocked at the downstair.

door. The lady answered truthfully that she didn't know. But the Moor said: "To me it looked like the squadron leader." "I don't know," she said, "whether it was he or someone else." The Moor held in his fury, though he burned with wrath.

He didn't want to do anything before he had spoken with the ensign, and so he went to him immediately and told him what had happened, and begged him to find out from the squadron leader what he could about the business. He, delighted with the way things were going, readily agreed to do so.

And so one day he spoke with the squadron leader while the Moor was standing in a place where he could see the two of them in conversation. As they talked of all sorts of things having nothing to do with the lady, the ensign laughed with huge gusto and made as if to show great surprise, gesturing a lot with his head and hands as if he heard some incredible tale. The Moor went to the ensign as soon as he saw the two separate, in order to know what the other had told him. The ensign, after making the Moor beg for a long time, finally said to him: "He hasn't hidden a thing from me. He says that he has enjoyed your wife every time that you've given him opportunity by being away. And, he says, on the last such time he was with her, she gave him the handkerchief which you gave her as a gift when you married her." The Moor thanked the ensign, and it seemed to him obvious that if the lady no longer had the handkerchief in her possession, all must be as the ensign had said.

And so one day, after they had dined, as he discussed various things with his lady, the Moor asked for the handkerchief. The poor woman, who had been so afraid of this question, turned all red in the face, and, in order to hide her blushes, which the Moor had already taken good notice of, she ran to her chest and pretended to look for it. After she had searched a good deal, she said: "I don't know why I can't find it now. Do you have it, by any chance?" "If I had it," he said, "why would I be asking you for it? But you will look for it more easily and comfortably some other time."

And, leaving her, the Moor began to think how he might kill his lady and the squadron leader at the same time in such a way that the guilt for her death would not be laid at his door. Thinking of this day and night, he couldn't prevent his lady from noticing that he was not the same toward her as before. She said to him several times: "What thing is bothering you? What is troubling you? You, who used to be the merriest person on earth, are now the most melancholy person alive." The Moor found various excuses in replying to his lady, but she was not at all easy in her mind.

Even though she knew that no misconduct on her part could have troubled the Moor so greatly, she feared nonetheless that through the excessive amount of lovemaking he engaged in with her, he had become bored. Sometimes she would say to the ensign's wife: "I don't know what to make of the Moor. He used to be so loving to me, and now, in I don't know how short a time, he's become quite another person. I'm greatly worried that I shall prove a warning to young women not to marry against their parents' wishes, and that Italian ladies will learn by my example not to be linked in marriage with the kind of man who is separated from us by nature, Heaven itself, and an entire way of life. But because I know he is on good terms with your husband and shares with him his most private affairs, I beg of you that, if you've learned anything from him that you can tell me about, you won't fail to help me." And as she said all this she wept uncontrollably.

The ensign's wife, who knew everything (since her husband wished to use her as a means to the death of the lady, though she had never willingly consented), did not dare, for the fear she had of her husband, to say a word of this thing to Disdemona. She said only: "Take care not to give your husband the least suspicion, and strive as hard as you can to make him realize your love and loyalty to him." "Why, so I do," Disdemona said, "but nothing helps."

The Moor, meanwhile, sought every way of confirming more certainly the very thing he did not want to discover. He begged the ensign to arrange matters in such a way that he could see the handkerchief in the squadron leader's possession, and, although this request put the scoundrel rather on the spot, he promised the Moor nonetheless to make every effort to give him the proof he desired.

The squadron leader had a woman in the house who made the most marvelous embroidery on fine linen. She, seeing the handkerchief and hearing that it belonged to the Moor's wife and that it was to be given back to her, undertook to make a copy of it before it was returned. While she was doing this, it struck the ensign that she had placed herself next to a window from which she could be seen by whoever passed by in the street. He made sure that the Moor saw this, who accordingly held it for certain that his utterly chaste lady was in fact an adulteress.

The Moor came to an agreement with the ensign to kill her and the squadron leader, and as the two of them discussed between them how it was to be done, the Moor implored the ensign that he would agree to be the one to kill the squadron leader, promising to remain eternally obliged to him for doing so. Although the ensign at first refused to undertake such a difficult and exceedingly dangerous thing, since the squadron leader was no less skillful than valorous, after having been begged repeatedly and bribed with a sufficient quantity of money, he was at length induced to say that he would undertake to tempt fortune.

One evening after these matters had been settled, as the squadron leader was leaving the house of a courtesan with whom he liked to solace himself, the night being dark, the ensign accosted him with sword in hand and directed a blow at his legs to cause him to fall, and in so doing cut the right thigh entirely through so that the poor man did indeed fall to the ground. The ensign was instantly upon him to finish him off. But the squadron leader, who was brave and accustomed to blood and death, drew his own sword and, wounded though he was, put himself on guard to defend his life and shouted in a loud voice: "Help! Murder!"

At this the ensign, hearing people running toward him, and among them some soldiers who were billeted in the neighborhood, took to his heels so as not to be taken there, and then, doubling back on his tracks, made it appear that he also was running toward the noise. Blending in among the others, and seeing the leg that had been lopped off, he judged that the squadron leader, if not virtually dead already, would die in any case of such a wound. And, although he rejoiced to himself at this, he nevertheless offered condolences to the squadron leader as if he had been his brother.

Next morning the news was all over the city, and came too

to the ears of Disdemona. She, loving as always, and not thinking that she might suffer harm from it, showed the greatest sorrow for what had happened. The Moor put the worst possible construction on her behavior. He went to find the ensign and said to him: "Do you know that my fool of a wife is in such a state about what has happened to the squadron leader that she is very nearly out of her mind?"

"What else could you expect," said the ensign, "since he is her very heart and soul?"

"Heart and soul, you say?" answered the Moor. "I'll tear her heart and soul right out of her body! I couldn't think myself a man if I didn't rid the world of such a depraved creature."

As they went on discussing alternatives, whether the lady should die by poison or the knife, and not coming to an agreement between them on one or the other, the ensign said: "A way has come into my head that should satisfy you and lead to no suspicion. Here it is. The house you occupy is very old, and the ceiling in your room is full of cracks. My idea is that we pummel Disdemona with a stocking filled with sand until she dies, since this way there will appear on her body no sign of a beating. Once she is dead we can cause part of the ceiling to cave in, and we can break the lady's head in such a way as to make it appear that a falling rafter smashed her skull and killed her. This way no one will suspect you, supposing instead that her death came about by accident."

This cruel advice pleased the Moor, and he waited only for a convenient opportunity, some night when he would share his bed with Disdemona. First he concealed the ensign in a dressing room that opened off their bedroom. Then the ensign, according to the plan they had made between them, made some sort of noise in the dressing room. Hearing this, the Moor said very suddenly to his wife: "Did you hear that noise?"

"Yes, I did," she said.

"Get up and see what it is," the Moor rejoined.

Poor Disdemona got up. As soon as she had come close to the dressing room, the ensign rushed out and, being strong and muscular, gave her a terrible blow in the small of her back with the stocking he had ready, so that the lady fell immediately, hardly able to draw her breath. With the little voice she had left she called on the Moor to help her. But he, leaping out of bed, said to her: "You most wicked of women! This is the reward for your unchastity. This is what they get who, pretending to love their husbands, put horns on their heads instead."

The poor lady, hearing this and sensing that her end was near—since the ensign had landed another blow—said that she called on divine justice to attest to her fidelity, since earthly justice failed to come to her aid. And as she called on God to help her, she was struck by a third blow and lay dead, slain by the impious ensign.

Then, putting her on the bed and smashing her skull, he and the Moor caused the ceiling of the room to cave in as they had planned between them, whereupon the Moor began to cry for help, that the house was falling down. At which cry the neighbors came running, and discovered the bed, and found the lady dead under the rafters. All were amazed and grieved at this, because her life had been so good.

On the following day Disdemona was buried with deep grieving on everybody's part. But God, the just examiner of all human souls, did not wish that such monstrous evil should go without suitable punishment. He decreed that the Moor, who had loved the lady more than his own life, seeing himself deprived of her, should begin to have such an intense longing for her that he went about like one who was out of his mind, searching for her in every imaginable place in the house. And coming to the conclusion that it was the ensign who had caused him to lose, along with the lady, every joy of his life and indeed his very being, he came to loathe the villain so intensely that he couldn't even bear to look at him. If he had not been afraid of the inviolable justice of the Venetian Seigniory, the Moor would have killed him right out in the open. But since he couldn't do so safely, he instead demoted the ensign and refused to let him serve any longer in his company, whereupon was born such a bitter enmity between them that it would be impossible to imagine one more immense or deadly.

On this score the ensign, that worst of all villains, turned all his thoughts to doing harm to the Moor. Seeking out the squadron leader, who had recovered by now and who got about on a wooden leg in place of the one that had been cut off, the ensign said to him: "The time has come for you to be revenged for your cut-off leg. If you'll come with me to Venice, I will tell you who the malefactor was. I don't dare talk about it here for many reasons. And I will testify for you in court."

The squadron leader, knowing himself to have been deeply wronged but not understanding the real truth of the matter, thanked the ensign and accompanied him to Venice. When they had arrived, the ensign told him that the Moor was the one who had cut off his leg because of an idea he had gotten into his head that he, the squadron leader, had lain with Disdemona, and that for this same reason the Moor had killed her and afterward spread the report of her having been killed by the falling ceiling.

The squadron leader, hearing this, accused the Moor before the Seigniory of having cut off his leg and of having killed the lady, and he called as his witness the ensign, who said that both things were true, which he knew because the Moor had told him everything and had tried to induce him to commit both crimes; and that, having then killed his wife, impelled by the bestial jealousy that had come into his head, the Moor had told to the ensign the manner in which he had done her in.

The Venetian Seigniory, upon learning of this cruel deed perpetrated by a barbarian foreigner on a Venetian citizen, issued orders for the Moor to be arrested in Cyprus and brought back to Venice, where through numerous tortures they tried to find out the truth. But he was able to endure all the tortures with his mightiness of spirit and denied everything so steadfastly that they could not get anything out of him. And although by his steadfastness he escaped death, he was, after being confined many days in prison, condemned to perpetual exile. There he was finally put to death by Disdemona's relatives, as he deserved.

The ensign went back to his own country, and, not being inclined to change his ways, accused a companion of his of having tried to get him, the ensign, to kill one of this fellow's enemies, a person of good birth. On the basis of this accusation the fellow was taken and put to the torture.

When he denied the truth of what his accuser had said, the ensign too was put to the torture in order that their stories might be compared. There he was so badly tortured that his internal organs ruptured. Afterward he was released from prison and taken home, where he died a miserable death. Thus did God avenge the innocence of Disdemona. And now that he was dead, the ensign's wife, who knew the whole story, told what had happened just as I have told you.

———————————

Gli Hecatommithi by Giovanni Battista Giraldi Cinthio was first published in Italy in 1565. This new translation is based on the edition of 1566.

Further Reading

Adamson, Jane. *"Othello" as Tragedy: Some Problems of Judgment and Feeling.* Cambridge and New York: Cambridge Univ. Press, 1980. Adamson finds the unity of *Othello* in the similarities between the problems of judgment and feeling that characters confront and those experienced by an audience of the play. We are made uncomfortable with our own desire for certainty as we see characters who, in theirs, urgently construe and misconstrue actions and personalities.

Bayley, John. "Love and Identity." *The Characters of Love: A Study in the Literature of Personality.* London: Constable, 1960. Examining the psychological and philosophical implications of Shakespeare's revision of G. B. Giraldi Cinthio's novella, Bayley sees the play as an intensely personal tragedy rooted in the difficulties of truly knowing another being. Both Desdemona and Othello reveal powerful conceptions of love but are tragically incapable of understanding any other kind of love or of being separated from their own sense of identity.

Boose, Lynda E. "Othello's Handkerchief: 'The Recognizance and Pledge of Love.'" *English Literary Renaissance* 5`(1975): 360–374. Boose discovers in the "strawberry spotted handkerchief" the motive forces of the play itself: the concerns with fidelity and justice. Examining Shakespeare's transformation of his source material and exploring Renaissance marriage customs, Boose finds that the handkerchief functions as an emblem of marital consummation, and that Othello's chosen role as judicial executioner derives from marriage laws and rituals that prescribe the death of a wife whose wedding sheets fail to provide proof of her bridal virginity.

Bradley, A. C. *"Othello." Shakespearean Tragedy,* 1904. Rpt., New York: St. Martin's Press, 1985. Bradley's deservedly influential study focuses on character: Othello is heroic, noble, not innately jealous but unreflective; Desdemona is passive, armed with nothing to oppose evil except endurance and forgiveness; and Iago is a liar, su-

premely evil, motivated by an unconscious longing for
power and superiority.

Cavell, Stanley. "Literature as the Knowledge of the Outsider." *The Claim of Reason: Wittgenstein, Scepticism,
Morality, and Tragedy.* New York: Oxford Univ. Press,
1979 Rpt. as "On *Othello,*" in *Shakespeare, the Tragedies:
New Perspectives,* ed. Robert B. Heilman. Englewood
Cliffs, N.J.: Prentice-Hall, 1984. Cavell sees the play enact-
ing the tragic implications of the individual's need for the
existence of—and acknowledgment by—another. Othello
needs Desdemona to confirm his image of himself but simultaneously has to reject Desdemona for exposing his
need. Othello's tragedy is then not the tragedy of a man
who lacks certainty but of one who knows too much—
about himself as dependent and imperfect—and is unable to confront that knowledge.

Coleridge, Samuel Taylor. *"Othello." Coleridge's Writings
on Shakespeare,* ed. Terence Hawkes. New York: G. P. Put-
nam's Sons, 1959. Coleridge regards Othello as a noble
and majestic figure, not jealous by nature but aroused by
offended honor, moral indignation, and regret at his discovery that Desdemona's virtue is apparently impure and
worthless. Coleridge views Iago as a "passionless character, all *will* and intellect," and, in a famous phrase, characterizes Iago's rationalizations of his hatred for Othello
as "the motive-hunting of motiveless malignity."

Doran, Madeleine. "Iago's 'If': An Essay on the Syntax of
Othello." In *The Drama of the Renaissance: Essays for
Leicester Bradner,* ed. Elmer M. Blistein. Providence, R.I.:
Brown Univ. Press, 1970. Rpt. and rev. as "Iago's 'If—':
Conditional and Subjunctive in *Othello.*" *Shakespeare's
Dramatic Language.* Madison: Univ. of Wisconsin Press,
1976. Analyzing Shakespeare's use of syntax to inform
the dramatic structure of *Othello,* Doran discovers two
dominant syntactic patterns counterpointed in the play:
conditional and declarative sentences. The conditionals
(which initiate every significant phase of the tragic
action) disrupt and finally destroy the world of Othello's
assurance. His absolutism and ultimately his whole being fall victim to the terrifying ambiguities released by
Iago's "if."

Empson, William. " 'Honest' in *Othello*." *The Structure of Complex Words*. New York: New Directions, 1951. Empson argues that Shakespeare's complex handling of the words "honest" and "honesty" (which appear over fifty times in the play) is central to an understanding of Iago's character and motivation. Shakespeare exploits the words' various possibilities of meaning, and a Renaissance audience, alert to the ironies and ambiguities of the words, would necessarily see Iago as less purely evil and more complexly human than most twentieth-century critics have allowed.

Gardner, Helen. "The Noble Moor." In *Proceedings of the British Academy* 41 (1956 for 1955): 189–205. Rpt. in *Shakespeare Criticism, 1935–60*, ed. Anne Ridler. London and New York: Oxford Univ. Press, 1963. As her title suggests, Gardner sees Othello as a noble and heroic figure in a play of poetic, intellectual, and moral beauty. The play's subject is not pride, egoism, or self-deception, but is, rather, loss of faith stemming from sexual jealousy. In *Othello* we are presented with the fall of a noble man from a great happiness to ruin, but a fall that affirms the value of the life and love that have been lost.

Garner, S. N. "Shakespeare's Desdemona." *Shakespeare Studies* 9 (1976): 233–252. Finding *Othello* to be among the "bleakest" of the tragedies, Garner traces Desdemona's tragic trajectory from her initial courage and confidence to her "appalling innocence" and passivity of the last two acts. Exactly like Othello, she never fully knows herself or her spouse, and both fail to "understand the way the world fosters their misperceptions."

Greenblatt, Stephen. "The Improvisation of Power." *Renaissance Self-Fashioning*. Chicago: Univ. of Chicago Press, 1980. In Greenblatt's suggestive cultural anthropology, *Othello* emerges as a play expressing the central social and psychic realities of the Renaissance. Iago's understanding that the self is something "fashioned" permits him the improvisational freedom to enter into the psychic structure of another and turn it to his advantage. Playing upon the ambivalence of Othello's relationship to Venetian society, Iago activates Othello's terrifying sexual anxieties and mistrust.

Heilman, Robert B. *Magic in the Web: Action and Language in "Othello."* Lexington, Ky.: Univ. of Kentucky Press, 1956. *Othello*, Heilman argues in his account of the play's imagery and dramatic action, is a "dramatic poem" about love. Othello's tragedy stems from his failure to recognize the transformative power of Desdemona's love. His histrionic bent, his self-pity, and his self-love allow him to be seduced by Iago's wit and reason, and he dies never knowing the true value of what he has lost.

Johnson, Samuel. *"Othello." Johnson on Shakespeare*, ed. Arthur Sherbo. *The Yale Edition of the Works of Samuel Johnson*, vol. 8. New Haven and London: Yale Univ. Press, 1969. Johnson praises the play for its moral qualities, its dramatic construction, and its vivid characterization. Othello is "boundless in his confidence, ardent in his affection, inflexible in his resolution, and obdurate in his revenge." Johnson also admires Desdemona's "soft simplicity" and finds her murder unbearable: "I am glad that I have ended my revisal of this dreadful scene. It is not to be endured."

Jones, Eldred. *Othello's Countrymen: The African in English Renaissance Drama*. London: Oxford Univ. Press, 1965. Jones surveys the Elizabethan knowledge of Africans and their representation on the stage and finds that *Othello* marks a significant departure from the traditional dramatic treatment of Moors: Shakespeare endows Othello with noble, human qualities, though the play invokes—in order to reject—racial stereotypes in the prejudice of Iago and Brabantio.

Kirsch, Arthur. "The Polarization of Erotic Love in *Othello." Modern Language Review* 73 (1978): 721–740. Rpt. as *"Othello." Shakespeare and the Experience of Love*. Cambridge and New York: Cambridge Univ. Press, 1981. According to Kirsch, Shakespeare in the play, and most deeply in Othello's character, explores the powerful and often paradoxical forces of erotic love. Drawing on both Christian and Freudian theories of desire, Kirsch understands *Othello* not as a tragedy of moral or psychological failure but as an enactment of the tragic potential of a human love born necessarily in vulnerability and need.

Knight, G. Wilson. "The *Othello* Music." *The Wheel of Fire: Interpretation of Shakespeare's Tragedy*, 1930. Rev. and enl., New York: Meridian, 1957. Iago's corrosive cynicism represents for Knight a "spirit of negation" that would destroy "the domesticity, the romance, the idealized humanity of the *Othello* world." But, while Iago succeeds in destroying the love and beauty of that world, his triumph is not complete. At the end Othello recovers his former dignity, rising above the chaos into which he has sunk and denying Iago an absolute victory.

Leavis, F. R. "Diabolic Intellect and the Noble Hero: A Note on *Othello.*" *Scrutiny* 6 (1937): 259–283. Rpt. in *The Common Pursuit*. London: Chatto and Windus, 1952; New York: New York Univ. Press, 1964. Leavis attacks what he calls the "Sentimentalists' Othello," promulgated by Coleridge, Johnson, and Bradley (see above). In place of their heroic and noble figure seduced by a supremely evil villain, he argues for an Othello driven by pride, sentimentality, and a lack of self-knowledge that makes him succumb "with an extraordinary promptness to suggestion."

Neely, Carol Thomas. "Women and Men in *Othello:* 'What Should Such a Fool / Do With So Good a Woman?'" *Shakespeare Studies* 10 (1977): 133–158. Rpt. in *The Woman's Part: Feminist Criticism of Shakespeare*, ed. Carolyn Ruth Swift Lenz, Gayle Greene, and Carol Thomas Neely. Urbana, Chicago, and London: Univ. of Illinois Press, 1980. Neely proposes that the play's central conflict is not between good and evil but between men and women. Unlike Shakespeare's comedies, where witty heroines are able to dispel male folly, *Othello* defines a world where male fantasies remain tragically unaffected by female wit and energy. Here the conflicts are never resolved, and at the end we do not celebrate the pairing of lovers but can only look at the dead bodies of Emilia, Desdemona, and Othello.

Orkin, Martin. "Othello and the 'Plain Face' of Racism." *Shakespeare Quarterly* 38 (1987): 166–188. Orkin traces attitudes toward race and color in Renaissance England and ways in which a "racist mythology inscribes critical responses to the play." In a final section, Orkin examines the specific case of the play as it is treated in the academic criticism of South Africa.

Rosenberg, Marvin. *The Masks of "Othello": The Search for the Identity of Othello, Iago, and Desdemona by Three Centuries of Actors and Critics*. Berkeley and Los Angeles: Univ. of California Press, 1961. Rosenberg's subtitle indicates the contents of his book. He examines the play on the stage from the eighteenth through the twentieth centuries, provides an overview of critical approaches, and attends to the ways in which the text has been reshaped for performance. In the two concluding chapters he argues against either symbolic or skeptical approaches to *Othello*, maintaining that *Othello*'s deep and complex humanity is most powerfully realized in the theater.

Snyder, Susan. "Beyond Comedy: *Romeo and Juliet* and *Othello*." *The Comic Matrix of Shakespeare's Tragedies*, esp. pp. 70–90. Princeton, N.J.: Princeton Univ. Press, 1979. Responding to the play's movement from an initial comic design to a fully developed tragic action, Snyder maintains that the power of *Othello* derives from Shakespeare's radical questioning of the fundamental assumption of romantic comedy: that self-definition and fulfillment can be achieved through union with another. The play enacts and explores the tragic implications of emotional ties that necessarily reveal the dependency and vulnerability that Iago exploits.

Spivack, Bernard. "Iago Revisited." *Shakespeare and the Allegory of Evil*. New York: Columbia Univ. Press, 1958. Finding no plausible motivation within the play for Iago's exuberant evil, Spivack discovers an explanation for his behavior not in Iago's psychology but in his literary ancestry in the medieval drama. Iago's logic and energy derive from the allegorical Vice of the morality plays, and Spivack explores the implications of this legacy for the moral dynamics of the play.

Stoll, E. E. *"Othello": An Historical and Comparative Study*, 1915. Rpt., New York: Haskell House, 1964. Stoll responds sharply to the psychological critics (notably Bradley, see above) who discuss the play's characters as if they were real people. Instead, Stoll argues for the primacy of plot, language, and stage conventions, and invites us to reconsider the play in light of the expectations and values of an Elizabethan audience.

Memorable Lines

A fellow almost damned in a fair wife.　　　(IAGO　1.1.22)

But I will wear my heart upon my sleeve
For daws to peck at.　　　(IAGO　1.1.66–67)

Keep up your bright swords, for the dew will rust them.
　　　(OTHELLO　1.2.60)

Rude am I in my speech,
And little blessed with the soft phrase of peace . . .
　　　(OTHELLO　1.3.83–84)

Wherein of antres vast and deserts idle,
Rough quarries, rocks, and hills whose heads touch
　　heaven . . .　　　(OTHELLO　1.3.142–143)

She swore, in faith, 'twas strange, 'twas passing strange,
'Twas pitiful, 'twas wondrous pitiful.
　　　(OTHELLO　1.3.162–163)

She loved me for the dangers I had passed,
And I loved her that she did pity them.
　　　(OTHELLO　1.3.169–170)

My noble Father,
I do perceive here a divided duty.
　　　(DESDEMONA　1.3.182–183)

Virtue? A fig! 'Tis in ourselves that we are thus or thus. Our
bodies are our gardens, to the which our wills are gardeners.
　　　(IAGO　1.3.322–324)

For I am nothing if not critical.　　　(IAGO　2.1.121)

To suckle fools and chronicle small beer.　　　(IAGO　2.1.160)

RODERIGO   She's full of most blessed condition.
IAGO   Blessed fig's end! The wine she drinks is made of
grapes.   (2.1.251–254)

I do suspect the lusty Moor
Hath leaped into my seat, the thought whereof
Doth, like a poisonous mineral, gnaw my innards.
(IAGO   2.1.296–298)

But men are men; the best sometimes forget. (IAGO   2.3.235)

Reputation, reputation, reputation! O, I have lost my reputation!   (CASSIO   2.3.256–257)

Divinity of hell!
When devils will the blackest sins put on,
They do suggest at first with heavenly shows,
As I do now.   (IAGO   2.3.344–347)

How poor are they that have not patience!
What wound did ever heal but by degrees?
(IAGO   2.3.364–365)

Good name in man and woman, dear my lord,
Is the immediate jewel of their souls.
Who steals my purse steals trash.   (IAGO   3.3.168–170)

O, beware, my lord, of jealousy!
It is the green-eyed monster which doth mock
The meat it feeds on.   (IAGO   3.3.178–180)

Poor and content is rich, and rich enough.   (IAGO   3.3.185)

To be once in doubt
Is once to be resolved.   (OTHELLO   3.3.193–194)

And yet, how nature erring from itself— (OTHELLO   3.3.243)

I'd whistle her off and let her down the wind
To prey at fortune.   (OTHELLO   3.3.278–279)

Trifles light as air
Are to the jealous confirmations strong
As proofs of Holy Writ.   (IAGO   3.3.338–340)

O, now, forever
Farewell the tranquil mind! Farewell content!
                                           (OTHELLO   3.3.363–364)

On horror's head horrors accumulate.   (OTHELLO   3.3.386)

Take note, take note, O world,
To be direct and honest is not safe.   (IAGO   3.3.393–394)

There's magic in the web of it.   (OTHELLO   3.4.71)

O, she will sing the savageness out of a bear.
                                           (OTHELLO   4.1.188–189)

But yet the pity of it, Iago! O, Iago, the pity of it, Iago!
                                           (OTHELLO   4.1.195–196)

It makes us or it mars us.   (IAGO   5.1.4)

It is the cause, it is the cause, my soul.   (OTHELLO   5.2.1)

Put out the light, and then put out the light.
                                           (OTHELLO   5.2.7)

Here is my journey's end, here is my butt
And very seamark of my utmost sail.
                                           (OTHELLO   5.2.276–277)

Cold, cold, my girl?
Even like thy chastity.   (OTHELLO   5.2.284–285)

I have done the state some service, and they know 't.
                                           (OTHELLO   5.2.349)

Then must you speak
Of one that loved not wisely but too well.
                                           (OTHELLO   5.2.353–354)

. . . of one whose hand,
Like the base Indian, threw a pearl away
Richer than all his tribe.   (OTHELLO   5.2.356–358)

Contributors

DAVID BEVINGTON, Phyllis Fay Horton Professor of Humanities at the University of Chicago, is editor of *The Complete Works of Shakespeare* (Scott, Foresman, 1980) and of *Medieval Drama* (Houghton Mifflin, 1975). His latest critical study is *Action Is Eloquence: Shakespeare's Language of Gesture* (Harvard University Press, 1984).

DAVID SCOTT KASTAN, Professor of English and Comparative Literature at Columbia University, is the author of *Shakespeare and the Shapes of Time* (University Press of New England, 1982).

JAMES HAMMERSMITH, Associate Professor of English at Auburn University, has published essays on various facets of Renaissance drama, including literary criticism, textual criticism, and printing history.

ROBERT KEAN TURNER, Professor of English at the University of Wisconsin–Milwaukee, is a general editor of the New Variorum Shakespeare (Modern Language Association of America) and a contributing editor to *The Dramatic Works in the Beaumont and Fletcher Canon* (Cambridge University Press, 1966–).

JAMES SHAPIRO, who coedited the bibliographies with David Scott Kastan, is Assistant Professor of English at Columbia University.

♣

JOSEPH PAPP, one of the most important forces in theater today, is the founder and producer of the New York Shakespeare Festival, America's largest and most prolific theatrical institution. Since 1954 Mr. Papp has produced or directed all but one of Shakespeare's plays—in Central Park, in schools, off and on Broadway, and at the Festival's permanent home, The Public Theater. He has also produced such award-winning plays and musical works as *Hair*, *A Chorus Line*, *Plenty*, and *The Mystery of Edwin Drood*, among many others.

THE BANTAM SHAKESPEARE COLLECTION

The Complete Works in 28 Volumes

Edited with Introductions by David Bevington

Forewords by Joseph Papp

Bantam is proud to announce an important new
edition of:

The Complete Works Of
William Shakespeare

Featuring:

*The complete texts with modern spelling and
punctuation

*Vivid, readable introductions by noted Shakespearean
  scholar David Bevington
*New forewords by Joseph Papp, renowned producer,
  director, and founder of the New York Shakespeare
  Festival
*Stunning, original cover art by Mark English, the
  most awarded illustrator in the history of the Society
  of Illustrators
*Photographs from some of the most celebrated
  performances by the New York Shakespeare Festival
*Complete source materials, notes, and annotated
  bibliographies based on the latest scholarships
*Stage histories for each play

ACCESSIBLE * AUTHORITATIVE * COMPLETE

SHAKESPEARE
The Complete works in 29 Volumes